D0930519

UNDERSTANDING
IAN McEWAN

Understanding Contemporary British Literature
Matthew J. Bruccoli, Series Editor

UNDERSTANDING
Ian
McEWAN

David Malcolm

University of South Carolina Press

Published in Columbia, South Carolina, by the
University of South Carolina Press

Manufactured in the United States of America

06 05 04 03 02   5 4 3 2 1

Library of Congress Cataloging-in-Publication Data

Malcolm, David, 1952–
   Understanding Ian McEwan / David Malcolm.
      p. cm. — (Understanding contemporary British literature)
   Includes bibliographical references and index.
   ISBN 1-57003-436-2
   1. McEwan, Ian—Criticism and interpretation. I. Title. II. Series.
PR6063.C4 Z78 2001
823'.914—dc21   2001003343

for Cheryl Alexander Malcolm

CONTENTS

EDITOR'S PREFACE

The volumes of *Understanding Contemporary British Literature* have been planned as guides or companions for students as well as good nonacademic readers. The editor and publisher perceive a need for these volumes because much of the influential contemporary literature makes special demands. Uninitiated readers encounter difficulty in approaching works that depart from the traditional forms and techniques of prose and poetry. Literature relies on conventions, but the conventions keep evolving; new writers form their own conventions—which in time may become familiar. Put simply, *UCBL* provides instruction in how to read certain contemporary writers—identifying and explicating their material, themes, use of language, point of view, structures, symbolism, and responses to experience.

The word *understanding* in the titles was deliberately chosen. Many willing readers lack an adequate understanding of how contemporary literature works; that is, what the author is attempting to express and the means by which it is conveyed. Although the criticism and analysis in the series have been aimed at a level of general accessibility, these introductory volumes are meant to be applied in conjunction with the works they cover. They do not provide a substitute for the works and authors they introduce, but rather prepare the reader for more profitable literary experiences.

M. J. B.

ACKNOWLEDGMENTS

I thank Zina Rohan, without whose generosity much of the research for this book could not have been done. I am also grateful to the University of Gdańsk, which provided funds for me to make visits to the British Library in London. I owe an intellectual debt to Professor Dr. Hab. Andrzej Zgorzelski of the University of Gdańsk. I thank the editorial staff of the University of South Carolina Press for their skillful work on the book.

I thank William and James Malcolm for their toleration. My thanks, as always, go to Cheryl Alexander Malcolm for her help, support, advice, and much else besides.

UNDERSTANDING
IAN McEWAN

CHAPTER ONE

Understanding
Ian McEwan

Ian McEwan is a professional writer who has lived by his writing for almost a quarter of a century. McEwan's family background, however, was anything but literary. He was born in 1948 in the British military town of Aldershot. His mother, Rose, was a local woman whose husband had died during World War II, leaving her with two children. After the war she married David McEwan, a Scottish sergeant major in the British Army. McEwan discusses his parents and their background in an interview published in 1978. Both had known difficult circumstances. His father had joined the British Army in the 1930s because of severe unemployment in Glasgow; life for a widow with two children after the war had been extremely hard.[1] The early years of McEwan's childhood were spent on British military bases in England, and then in Singapore and Libya. When he was about eight years old, his father became an officer (in British terms, a social as well as a military promotion). It was in Libya that McEwan claims to have had his first sense of the force of history and politics. At the time of Britain's and France's invasion of Egypt in 1956, supposedly to maintain control of the Suez Canal, British military families were gathered together in armed camps for their own protection. Watching his father organizing matters, "a service revolver strapped around his waist," made McEwan understand "for the first time that political events were real and affected people's lives—they were not just stories in the papers that grown-ups read."[2]

In 1978 McEwan described his father as "handsome" and "domineering" and his mother, on the other hand, as "a very gentle woman, very easily tyrannized."[3] From 1959 to 1966 McEwan attended a government-funded boarding school for boys in Sussex in the south of England. He studied English and French at the then recently founded University of Sussex from 1967 to 1970. At university he developed literary ambitions, writing plays and adapting a Thomas Mann short story for television. "The desire to be a writer really did precede the material," he confesses. In 1970, having graduated from Sussex, he took the opportunity to earn an M.A. degree at the also newly established University of East Anglia, a degree that offered him the, at that time unusual, possibility of submitting "a little bit of fiction" to make up about a sixth of the course work for the master's degree.[4] (This was not a creative writing course such as exist now in many U.S. universities, but it was something like it.) Much later, in 1998, McEwan praised the supervisor of the fiction element in his course work, the eminent novelist and American literature specialist, Malcolm Bradbury.[5] McEwan says that he read a lot of modern fiction at East Anglia, "Mailer, Nabokov, and so on." He also wrote about twenty-five short stories, several of which were included in his two volumes of short stories, *First Love, Last Rites* and *In between the Sheets*.

After East Anglia and after a trip by bus "on the hippy trail" to Afghanistan in 1972, McEwan followed a literary career.[6] Even before the trip to Afghanistan, he had been able to sell stories to good literary journals, and Secker and Warburg, a major publisher, had asked him to expand an early short story, "Homemade," into a novel. But from the mid-1970s his career took off. Since 1975 he has published two volumes of short stories (*First Love, Last Rites* [1975] and *In between the Sheets* [1978]) and seven novels—*The Cement Garden* (1978), *The Comfort of Strangers* (1981), *The Child*

UNDERSTANDING IAN MCEWAN

in Time (1987), *The Innocent* (1989), *Black Dogs* (1992), *Enduring Love* (1997), and *Amsterdam* (1998). He has published one substantial collection of stories for children, *The Daydreamer* (1995). He has always found publishers for his work, has always been taken seriously by reviewers (even when they disapproved of his fiction), and has won many prizes and much prestige in the course of a productive twenty-five years. *First Love, Last Rites* won the Somerset Maugham Award in 1975; *The Comfort of Strangers* was shortlisted for the Booker Prize in 1981; his movie script *The Ploughman's Lunch* won the *Evening Standard* Award for the best screenplay of 1983; McEwan was made a Fellow of the Royal Society of Literature in 1984; *The Child in Time* won the Whitbread Novel of the Year Award in 1987; he was awarded an honorary Litt.D. by the University of Sussex in 1989; *Black Dogs* was shortlisted for the Booker Prize in 1993; and *Amsterdam* won the Booker Prize in 1998. Films have been made of *The Cement Garden*, *The Comfort of Strangers*, and *The Innocent*, and McEwan himself has achieved success as a scriptwriter both in the British movie and television industry and in Hollywood.

In 1982 he married Penny Allen, described as "journalist turned alternative thinker." This marriage seems to have been very happy (McEwan certainly presented it as such), although it ended in a bitter divorce in 1997.[7] Both partners have signed a legal agreement preventing either of them from disclosing "the secrets of the marriage," and McEwan through his lawyers has been strict in enforcing this agreement.[8] He married his second wife, Annalena McAfee, a literary journalist on the *Financial Times*, in 1997. McEwan has two children from his marriage with Allen. Despite the upheavals in his private life, a recent article on McEwan presents him as a happy, worldly, fashionably dressed, reasonably prosperous professional upper-middle-class man.[9]

McEwan has always been taken seriously by critics and scholars, although they have not always liked his books. Individual chapters of this study set out critical responses to his various texts. But it will be useful to give the overall story here. Kiernan Ryan summarizes "the received wisdom" about McEwan's work as it was in 1994.

> McEwan started out the seventies as a writer obsessed with the perverse, the grotesque, the macabre. The secret of his appeal lay in his stylish morbidity, in the elegant detachment with which he chronicled acts of sexual abuse, sadistic torment and pure insanity. But towards the close of the decade his writing underwent a marked evolution as a result of his increasing involvement with feminism and the peace movement. His politically committed work for the cinema and television turned out to be a watershed in his career, from which his fiction emerged transformed. The claustrophobic menace of the stories and his first two novels gave way in the eighties to a more mature engagement with the wider world of history and society. The clammy feel of impending evil which fouled the atmosphere of his early fiction was dispelled by an emerging apprehension of the power of love and the possibility of redemption.[10]

Ryan goes on to stress that this version of McEwan's career to 1994 obscures the continuities in his work. He does not simply become a right-thinking, social prophet in the mid-1980s; dark nightmares still haunt his work.[11] But the story is persuasive, and it is supported by McEwan himself. As early as 1977, after completing *The Cement Garden*, he recalls, "I felt I had written myself into too tight a corner; I had made deliberate use of material too restricted to allow me to write about the ideas that had interested me for some years." The specific interest he refers to is in the "Woman's Movement."[12] In an interview from 1985 he says that a step into greater social and political awareness "was something I intended, because I had begun to feel rather trapped by the kind of thing I had been writing. I had been labeled as the chronicler of comically exaggerated psychopathic states of mind or of adolescent anxiety, snot and pimples. . . . In writing *The Imitation Game* I stepped out into the world."[13]

McEwan emphasizes the direct social and political concerns of his 1983 oratorio, *Or Shall We Die?*, in his Introduction to the text, and most critical responses to *The Child in Time* from 1987 note the way in which McEwan has broadened his concerns from the hermetically and luridly psychopathological world of the early fiction to achieve a new maturity in his examination of social issues and his endorsement of the possibilities of redemption. *The Child in Time*, with its positive, adult ending, does mark a point of change in McEwan's fiction. Thereafter, in *The Innocent* and in *Black Dogs*, although there are nightmarish episodes and events, the vision of the world seems more benign. Certainly, both novels are much more engaged with the social, political, and historical than *The Cement Garden* or *The Comfort of Strangers*.

The story changes, however, after the mid-1990s. McEwan's latest fiction, *Enduring Love* and *Amsterdam*, shows the author moving in a different direction from the one sketched out in the received wisdom of 1994. *Enduring Love* is a return to the hectic, closed-in, psychologically disturbed world of the early fiction, while *Amsterdam* is a thoroughly sour account of human shabbiness and frailty without a single moment of redemption. (Indeed, in *Enduring Love*, too, the power of love that could save characters and maybe even the nation in *The Child in Time* has become a terribly fragile thing, or a matter of pathological obsession.) Critics have noted some of this change, but it has not diminished McEwan's stature. He remains a major British novelist of the late twentieth century and a highly respected professional writer.

McEwan started writing and publishing fiction in the mid-1970s, on the threshold of a period of particular dynamism in the development of the novel in Britain. His short stories and novels were written and published in the context of the changes, both perceived and real, that shaped British fiction in the last twenty or so years of the twentieth century.

It is argued by many commentators that the late 1970s and early 1980s mark an important point of departure in contemporary British fiction, the clear emergence of a new generation or grouping of writers and of new concerns in fiction. There are four main features of the new literary fiction of the 1980s and 1990s. These are a fascination with history, with historical events and processes both in the distant and more immediate (sometimes very immediate) past; an interest in settings abroad, outside the British Isles, or in characters and experiences from outside that geographical area; a considerable prominence of genre mixture; and metafictional interests (that is, fiction that constantly reminds the reader it is fiction and also addresses the problems and possibilities of storytelling and narrative generally).[14]

UNDERSTANDING IAN MCEWAN

Where does McEwan stand in relation to this particularly dynamic period in British fiction? The answer is that he is firmly part of the dominant trends in 1980s and 1990s fiction, but also shows interesting divergences from them. In terms of his contemporaries' concern with history, McEwan's novels and other writing both share that interest and also focus on the world in a rather different way. The interest in history and in the connected area of public, national life is very marked in *The Child in Time*, which is, in many ways, a head-on engagement with the dominant political ideology of 1980s Britain and a denunciation of what Conservative Party politics have brought (and might yet bring) to the country. *The Innocent* is a kind of historical novel, a careful reconstruction of mid-1950s Berlin and of an English frame of mind from that time. Its depiction of a skirmish in the cold war and of the power and dynamism of mid-twentieth-century U.S. popular culture and of the United States itself as a political entity forms a very important part of the text, interweaving with the novel's psychological concerns. In *Black Dogs*, of course, the historical permeates the whole text. Postwar British communism, the legacy of World War II, Poland in 1981, the fall of the Berlin Wall—all these are the conditions and the circumstances of June and Bernard's failed marriage and of Jeremy's fascinated pursuit of the causes of that failure. Clearly, McEwan's screenplays *The Imitation Game* and *The Ploughman's Lunch* are key texts in which McEwan in the mid-1980s starts most certainly to move from the almost asocial and ahistorical psychological concerns of his early fiction toward an engagement with wider historical and social issues.

But the picture is not as simple as that. The chapters in this study on *The Cement Garden* and *The Comfort of Strangers* indicate that these novels are not wholly without a sense of history and wider society. Although it would be wrong to overemphasize this, the children's slide into anarchy in *The Cement Garden* and their escape from all authority and traditional moral and social standards suggest a certain interpretation of recent British history and social development. In *The Comfort of Strangers*, Colin and Mary attempt to cut themselves off from the wider world of the past of the city they visit, only to be confronted and destroyed by figures from that world and from that past. One should also note that McEwan's two most recent novels, *Enduring Love* and *Amsterdam*, demonstrate a complicated position toward the historical and the social. In *Enduring Love*, the characters are almost entirely removed from these settings. Joe, Clarissa, and Jed inhabit a world that is almost completely without the social, political, and historical determinants of that of *The Child in Time*, *The Innocent*, and *Black Dogs*. If they are there (and it would be difficult to write any novel that was quite without them), they are of secondary importance to the novel's presentation of Joe's and Jed's minds. *Amsterdam* is social satire, and that satire has a political dimension. Also, because it is a satire focusing largely on the members of a particular generation of men, coming to age in the 1960s and 1970s, profiting from the 1980s, and securely ensconced in positions of authority by the 1990s, it has a certain historical dimension. Yet the focus in this novel, too, is on the present and on certain psychological states. How this aspect of McEwan's fiction will develop in the new century is far from clear.

The cosmopolitanism that is so much a part of British fiction in the 1980s and 1990s is something that weaves in and out of McEwan's fiction. It is clearly there in *The Comfort of Strangers* with its quasi-Venetian setting and its allusions to German literature. *The Innocent*

UNDERSTANDING IAN MCEWAN

and *Black Dogs* flaunt their cosmopolitanism. *The Child in Time*, however, is a late-twentieth-century "condition-of-England" novel, and it would be difficult to imagine more hermetically English novels than *The Cement Garden* and *Enduring Love*. Heathrow Airport is as near as Joe comes to abroad. *Amsterdam* reaches its climax in the Dutch city of that name, but the foreign setting is only a backdrop to concerns the characters bring from Britain. It could really be anywhere with lax euthanasia regulations. Indeed, in this matter McEwan at times echoes the stubborn provincialism of many contemporary British novels. Graham Swift's and Peter Ackroyd's fiction, as well as the firmly Scottish focus of Alasdair Gray's, James Kelman's, Irvine Welsh's, and (in part) Alan Warner's novels, are cases in point.

McEwan does not engage in much genre mixture, certainly not by the wildly eclectic standards of some of his contemporaries (Swift, Ackroyd, Carter, and Winterson are good examples). There are, to be sure, genre shifts in *The Cement Garden*, *The Comfort of Strangers*, and *The Child in Time*, but even *The Innocent* mixes psychological fiction with only one other genre, that of espionage fiction. The short stories, *Black Dogs*, *Enduring Love*, and *Amsterdam* are primarily examples of psychological fiction, like *The Cement Garden* and *The Comfort of Strangers* largely without the admixture of other genres. In this respect, McEwan stands out very clearly from many other 1980s and 1990s novelists.

Metafictional concerns, that is, self-reflexive concerns with fiction's possibilities and problems, permeate British fiction in the 1980s and 1990s. McEwan's fiction stands in complex and interesting relationship to this tendency. He is certainly frequently concerned with literature itself as a topic, and the difficulties, possibilities, and complexities of giving an account of things and of telling stories in general. Such concerns, however, in his later fiction at least, remain on the level of topic (that is, they are discussed as subject matter) without penetrating the technical level of the text itself (that is, they are not embodied on the level of narration, language, narrative organization, or genre, among others). Thus, *The Cement Garden* critically looks at maturation narratives and other classic texts by depicting regression rather than maturity and by placing the heart of darkness in England and not in an exotic locale. *The Comfort of Strangers* can be seen as an attempt to rewrite the gothic novel and also Thomas Mann's famous novella, *Der Tod in Venedig* (Death in Venice). *The Child in Time* is permeated by motifs of relativity of perception, while *The Innocent*, too, presents a world in which it is difficult to give an account of anything and in which characters are surrounded by fictions. Both *Black Dogs* and *Enduring Love* are centrally concerned with different versions of the same occurrences, although in both cases—in *Black Dogs*, in the final account of the incident of the dogs; in *Enduring Love*, in the way in which Joe is shown to have been right all along—the novels demonstrate that it *is* finally possible to give a worthwhile, accurate record of what happens.

However, McEwan does not always embody these concerns in his texts themselves. He does so in his early novels—through language in *The Cement Garden* and *The Comfort of Strangers*. Jack's overformal vocabulary undermines character probability at times and makes him seem a creation of the novel's author, rather than anything like a real human being. The narrator's extremely formal language in *The Comfort of Strangers* draws attention to the manner of telling rather than to what is being described or recounted. Narration, language, and a degree of genre mixture in *The Child in Time* bring the text itself as text forcibly to the reader's attention, but such elements become very weak in *The Innocent* and *Black Dogs* and virtually disappear in *Enduring Love*. The narrative of *Black Dogs* is self-advertisingly intricate, and it is a highly allusive literary text, but on the level of narration and genre it is rather traditional and transparent (that is, technique does not draw attention to itself). The same is true of *Enduring Love* and *Amsterdam*. Technically, these are both texts operating within well-established, non-experimental traditions. Indeed, *Amsterdam*, apart from Clive's experiences with the confusions of a police identity parade, ignores metafictional concerns altogether. In many ways, *Black Dogs* can serve as a representative of McEwan's focus up to now on metafictional issues. There are problems in giving accounts, he suggests: the reader must remember that he/she gains access to reality through texts that are not transparent windows, but particular shapings of events through language, narrative, and genre; however, accounts can be given. In his contribution to a symposium on fiction published in the *New Review* in 1978, McEwan argues that "there can surely be no more mileage to be had from demonstrating yet again through self-enclosed 'fictions' that reality is words and words are lies. There is no need to be strangled by that particular loop—the artifice of fiction can be taken for granted."[15] Here he does not foresee that a fascination with precisely this issue will come to dominate a great deal of British fiction in the 1980s and 1990s, but he does capture the path his own fiction will follow, certainly from *The Innocent* on. In his work there is an awareness of all the epistemological problems of providing accurate records of events, but also a reluctance to embody these on a textual level and a willingness to provide the reader with traditional, unproblematic narratives.

There are four other issues that any critic of McEwan's work must focus on. These are his presentation of women, and the role of feminist concerns in his fiction; his concern with rationalism and science; the moral perspective of his texts; and the fragmentariness of his novels.

In the early 1980s an interest in the Women's Movement clearly shaped some of the subject matter and social and moral outlook of McEwan's fiction. This has been well documented by critics, not always with approval, and acknowledged by McEwan himself. His writing certainly shows some complex developments in terms of its interest in women characters and of their roles in that fiction. This interest does not simply emerge in the 1980s, but is there in the short fiction from the mid- to late-1970s as well. "Homemade," "Pornography," and "Dead As They Come" all present traditional male attitudes of control, domination, and exploitation toward women in extreme and revealing forms. *The Cement Garden* is partly organized around a complex polarization of male and female, with emphasis on male beastliness. In *The Comfort of Strangers* Robert is a lurid embodiment of male arrogance and worse toward women. Colin and Mary, liberal, intelligent, and sensitive, are sucked into a diseased patriarchal nightmare. Later, the patriarchal obsessions that drive the characters in "Homemade" or "Dead As They Come" are echoed in Leonard's fantasies in *The Innocent*, fantasies that almost destroy, and certainly disrupt, his relationship with Maria. While any feminist concern in *The Ploughman's Lunch* is muted, *The Imitation Game* and *Or Shall We Die?* are ringingly feminist pieces.

From a feminist point of view, *The Child in Time* (supposedly McEwan's bold step into social engagement and maturity) is a quite mixed text. In it, female figures—Stephen's wife, Julie; his absent daughter; his friend Thelma; his mother; perhaps the prime minister him/herself (the gender is never given)—play enormously important roles, but they are all secondary to Stephen. Further, as Adam Mars-Jones has pointed out, McEwan has Stephen usurp female roles on ~~l occasions in the text.[16] Most notably, he delivers his own second child, on whom so much hope hangs for the world of the novel. Is one dealing here with a man stealing a woman's potential, or a man becoming sensitive to women's experiences? The question remains open.

In *Black Dogs* the contrast between June's metaphysical view of the world and Bernard's rational, materialist one is seen partly as a male-female clash, and the novel remains balanced between the two viewpoints. But in *Enduring Love*, there is little doubt that Joe's rational materialism is superior to Clarissa's vague emotionalism, and, indeed, her reliance on feeling over reason echoes the habits of mind of a psychopath. *Amsterdam* deals with women by having most of them dead or absent, barely presented figures on the margins of the story, and Garmony's transvestism suggests that the novel is more concerned with male attitudes toward being male than toward real women as such.

In fact, McEwan's supposed feminism has severe limitations in his fiction. It is clearly there in *The Imitation Game* and *Or Shall We Die?,* and he is a writer who is an expert at writing about a kind of diseased patriarchal mentality and how men are brutal toward women in deed and thought. But the women he presents are often far from admirable themselves. The penis-excising ladies in "Pornography" are at best ambiguous (although O'Byrne, perhaps, deserves what he gets), while many of McEwan's female figures echo very traditional feminine stereotypes. They are often victims, it should be noted, or mothers, mystics, and emotionalists, like June in *Black Dogs*. Even Thelma in *The Child in Time* is a traditionally sibylline wise woman, and her physics seems less science than white magic, while Clarissa in *Enduring Love* is beautiful but no use at all in facing off the stalker.

A summary of the stories of McEwan's novels will show that he is very concerned with the role of the irrational in his characters' lives. From the early short stories the reader sees characters driven by desires and emotions that they cannot control or really analyze themselves. For example, in *The Cement Garden* Jack is a mass of confused feelings—resentment toward his father, love of his mother that is coupled with a desire to be free of her, sexual fascination with his beautiful sister. In *The Comfort of Strangers*, Colin and Mary, so sensible, so balanced, drift half-willingly, half-aware, into Robert's sexual obsessions. *The Child in Time* charts Stephen's obsessive pursuit of his lost child, and in Charles Darke presents a man driven by a desire to revert to childhood that makes him abandon career, wealth, and adulthood. In *The Innocent* the sensible Leonard discovers love, but also discovers the darker side of emotions—dangerous fantasy, hatred, violence, and brutal murder. June in *Black Dogs* is a benign mystic, but her beliefs are highly subjective and beyond reasonable proof, while the point about Jed in *Enduring Love* is precisely that reason and evidence have no effect on his passion. In this latter novel, too, even the rational Joe has irrational sides to his character.

UNDERSTANDING IAN MCEWAN

As a counterbalance to the severe irrationality of many of his characters, McEwan does show the possibilities of reason, rationality, and, above all, science. In *The Child in Time* Thelma the physicist's calm voice perhaps influences Stephen in his crucial encounter with his wife in her cottage after his vision outside The Bell pub. In *Black Dogs* Bernard's stubborn materialism and rationality is given space and force equal to June's mysticism. In *Enduring Love* the scientific, rational Joe, for all his flaws, is the voice and the perspective the novel endorses. This voice seems lacking in *Amsterdam,* however. Garmony has uncontrollable transvestite desires that destroy his career, while Clive is an egoist who cannot place a woman's life above his own artistic aims. Vernon's case is more complex, but even he is driven by a desire for success that makes him deaf to rational argument.

Garmony's transvestism illustrates McEwan's fascination with taboo subjects throughout his fiction. Critics have always been fond of noticing incidences in his novels of incest, child abuse, fetishism, bondage, macabre combinations of sex and murder, infantile regression, and corpse dismemberment, at the serious end of the scale, and casual transvestism, obsessive masturbation, public nose picking, and a fascination with body fluids and odors, at the less serious end. As a result, one of the principal concerns of the McEwan critic must be the moral perspective of his texts. How do his novels and short stories judge the forms of behavior they depict? Overall, McEwan's career shows a trajectory from quite extreme moral relativism toward a rather clear moral focus. It is very hard to detect any moral judgment of characters and situations in the short stories and in *The Cement Garden.* The characters are what they are and they do what they do. Even the most horrible of crimes and acts that would usually be categorized as perverse are recounted without a breath of moral censure. Any moral judgment seems left to the reader. *The Comfort of Strangers* is complex in this respect. Robert and Caroline are sexually perverse murderers, but there is a lack of overt condemnation of their acts from the protagonists and the narrator. The loss of Colin, however, is surely meant to sadden the reader, although one is also perhaps meant to have a sense that he has partly brought his death on himself.

Moral positions become more obvious in the screenplays of the early 1980s. Cathy's treatment in *The Imitation Game* is meant to outrage the viewer. But even in *The Ploughman's Lunch*, criticism of Penfield is implied rather than stated openly. He glances at his watch during his mother's funeral, and most viewers and readers will surely respond to this act with distaste, but a different moral viewpoint from Penfield's is only indirectly given in his poet friend, in Ann Barrington, and in the women of the peace camp. However, a moral and social position is made very clear in *The Child in Time*. Stephen (and his father) leave one in no doubt that the state of Britain in the novel is a diseased one. Even Charles's regressive behavior (the kind of thing that is rarely criticized in McEwan's work) is seen as no way out of the malaise that is contemporary British life. Jeremy, the narrator in *Black Dogs*, passes frequent moral judgments—on the fascist skinheads in Berlin, on Majdanek, on Bernard and June, and on the dogs themselves. Bernard and June, too, have lots of views on various topics, views that the narrator takes very seriously. The novel itself ends with speculation about the poisoned nature of the European past and future. The moral focus of *Enduring Love* could scarcely be clearer. It is, for all the novel's complexities, a long and absorbing defense of rationalism and materialism. It is virtually a didactic novel.

However, the trajectory is not a perfect one. Both *The Innocent* and *Amsterdam* complicate the matter. *The Innocent* is a morally relativist text. The cold war is rarely seen in the novel as a clear-cut crusade against evil, but rather as an enormously complicated boys' game. Treachery exists in the world of the novel but is not condemned. Blake, MacNamee, Glass, Maria, and Leonard all commit betrayals of different kinds. Otto is a drunken lout, but hardly evil. Killing and dismembering him are accidents and are not overtly condemned in the novel. They are rather presented as things anyone could find him/herself involved in under the right (or wrong) circumstances. The situation in *Amsterdam* is equally complicated. Clive and Vernon are punished for their stupidity and moral baseness, as is the hypocritical Garmony. But George, who is equally corrupt, wins out in the end and sets off to start an affair with Vernon's widow. The whole world of the novel (largely restricted, let it be noted, to men) is morally corrupt, but there is no real voice of honesty or honor to provide a moral standard within the novel. That world echoes the amoral one of the early short stories and early novels.

The final issue in McEwan criticism concerns the fragmentariness of his novels. Jason Cowley argues in his 1998 essay on McEwan that his novels are "narratives of moments: a series of imaginative set pieces which seldom coagulate into a fully realized work."[17] This issue only emerges with McEwan's longer novels, that is, from *The Child in Time* onward. The short stories and the two early novels are themselves so short that the question of their fragmentariness does not arise. But in *The Child in Time*, the loss of the daughter in the supermarket and Stephen's climbing Charles's tree are two separate episodes that stand out from the main text by virtue of their emotional charge and their narrative completeness. The same applies to Otto's dismemberment in *The Innocent*, and to the ballooning accident and gun-buying episodes in *Enduring Love*. One might argue that *Black Dogs* is made up of a series of discrete episodes of this kind—for example, Jeremy and Bernard's visit to Berlin, the incident of the scorpion, the story of the black dogs itself. These all seem very powerful mininarratives, with beginnings, middles, and ends and with suitably intriguing complications and climaxes.

However, the degree to which such episodes are unintegrated fragments in McEwan's novels can be exaggerated. They are almost all carefully integrated into their respective novels. The shock of losing a daughter is emphasized by that episode's slightly separate status within *The Child in Time*. The same is true of the ballooning accident in *Enduring Love*. The incident destabilizes the characters' lives, and that needs to be underlined. The account of Otto's dismemberment vividly and physically demonstrates the horror that decent, likable people can find themselves involved in. The tree-climbing episode in *The Child in Time* or that of gun buying in *Enduring Love* very clearly mark the disturbance and dislocation of the main characters' lives. The fragmentariness of *Black Dogs* is perhaps the very point of the novel. It suggests the reader is surrounded by stories that try to recount and make sense of a whole mass of events. One wonders sometimes whether readers would notice the fragmentariness of some of McEwan's novels if he had not started off as a short-story writer.

McEwan is at present in his early fifties. He is a writer who has produced a substantial body of work, mostly in the novel, but also in other kinds and media. One cannot know what the overall picture of his fiction will be in twenty or thirty years, let alone the final verdict on it. One does not know what he will do next. All the critic can do is observe certain patterns and continuities in his work to date. The most important of these appear to be a movement in and out of metafictional concerns, a complex interest in feminist issues, an interplay of moral relativism and moral judgment, and an enduring love of psychological fiction. At any rate, McEwan has already written two small masterpieces, *The Cement Garden* and *The Comfort of Strangers*, and one very distinguished full-length novel, *The Innocent*. The rest of his work is simply very good.

CHAPTER TWO

The Short Stories
First Love, Last Rites and
In between the Sheets

In a 1983 interview, McEwan says of the short fiction he wrote and published in the mid to late 1970s: "I took the stories very seriously and worked on them very slowly, and I would always want to stand by them."[1] These short stories are worth paying attention to for several reasons. They established McEwan as a young writer of some importance; critics took and take them very seriously; McEwan himself clearly has a substantial regard for them; and they point in many different and complex ways toward the later novels. In addition, several of them are interesting and powerful pieces of work in their own right, and the collections themselves form striking and unified wholes.

The stories have often had their admirers and have rarely met with indifference. In his 1996 study of McEwan's fiction, Jack Slay, Jr., devotes a considerable amount of space to his discussion of the two collections.[2] In a general article on McEwan and his work from December 1998, Jason Cowley argues forcefully that McEwan's career since the short stories has been a decline and retreat from "ambition" and "experimentation," from the "elusive and pure" quality and the "imaginative brio" of those early stories.[3] *First Love, Last Rites* (1975) won approving mentions in the *Partisan Review* and in the *Sewanee Review* when the collection first appeared in the U.S., and Hermione Lee's review of *In between the Sheets* (1978) in the *New Statesman* is quite positive: she writes that these "seven elegantly gruesome accounts of derelict and perverted lives cannot be dismissed after the first *frisson*: their peculiar images of pain and loss seem, retrospectively, to grow in depth." In the *Observer* the same critic declares of the later collection that in it McEwan shows himself "an immaculate short story writer who casts a cold, exact eye on desire, embarrassment and estrangement. And he is very funny." Other responses have been more mixed, however. In the *New York Times Book Review*, Julian Moynahan does not conceal his distaste for the subject matter and what he sees as the derivative fashionableness of that subject matter in *In between the Sheets*. The response of the reviewer in the *Times Literary Supplement* is more mixed, but scarcely approving. According to Caroline Blackwood, McEwan "is an original writer. His descriptions of desolate urban landscapes are very vivid. He can create a memorable atmosphere of menace. But he disgusts at a cost, for his determination to shock can make his dialogue absurdly tortured and the stories too contrived."[4] Yet the short stories have important defenders; substantial figures in the British literary-critical establishment, like Christopher Ricks and Ian Hamilton, make their regard for them quite clear.[5]

Some critics suggest that the subject matter of McEwan's short stories is quite limited. This is not entirely true. Several, but by no means all, of those in *First Love, Last Rites* are concerned with adolescents, children, and young adults. In "Homemade," an adult narrator recounts how as a fourteen-year-old he achieved sexual initiation of a sort by having sexual intercourse with his younger sister. "The Last Day of Summer" is narrated by an orphaned twelve-year-old boy, who observes the life of the adults around him and also undergoes further experiences of loss and death. "Conversation with a Cupboard Man" presents the psychologically traumatic experiences and their consequences of a young man's treatment by his obsessive and then indifferent mother. The subject matter of "Disguises" is similar. Here a young boy who is being brought up by his aunt is dragged into the aunt's fantasy world, including her transvestite games. "First Love, Last Rites," on the other hand, is told by a narrator at the brink of adulthood, whose relationship with his silent, guarded girlfriend becomes strangely stagnant and then seems to revive after an encounter with a pregnant rat. "Butterflies" also involves a child, but the center of the story is rather the unhappy and isolated young man who sexually abuses and murders her, while "Cocker at the Theatre" (perhaps the weakest of the stories) has adult protagonists, actors in a sex show, two of whom, instead of only simulating intercourse on stage, actually have sex during a rehearsal, much to the consternation of the director and choreographer. The protagonists of "Solid Geometry" are also adults, although the chilly, self-absorbed husband who destroys his wife physically, emotionally, and finally by magic has a certain immature egoism which recalls adolescence.

Children are present, too, in the stories of *In between the Sheets*, although, as in "Butterflies," they are not the central figures or narrators. In "Two Fragments: March 199–," which is set in a postapocalyptic future England, the narrator is much concerned with his young daughter and her life in the desolate urban wasteland, but the story is told from his point of view instead of hers. A father's concern for his daughter is also central to "In between the Sheets." Here the text actually shifts briefly to the daughter's point of view but is largely given through the father's. He is divorced from his wife, lonely, and with a strong sense of failure and inadequacy. When his fourteen-year-old daughter visits him with her girlfriend,

THE SHORT STORIES

who is a dwarf, Stephen overhears what he thinks are his daughter's orgasmic cries from the bedroom she is sharing with her friend. At the story's end, however, he realizes that he is probably wrong and recovers a sense of his daughter's childhood innocence.

Adult experiences are central to the stories in this collection. "To and Fro" is an attempt to evoke the rich, pleasant, private world of sleeping in a lover's bed, and to contrast that with the rather dull, conflict-ridden, superficial one of work in an office. "Pornography," "Dead As They Come," and "Psychopolis" are all set among adults, and at least two of them deal with adult sexual deviance of some sort. "Pornography" tells the story of the brutish O'Byrne, who works in his brother's pornographic bookstore. He is having affairs with two nurses at the same hospital, treats one of them with some cruelty, infects them both with venereal disease, and then has his penis cut off by the two women (an experience that he realizes at the last moment he is enjoying!). "Dead As They Come" is narrated by a wealthy businessman who falls in love with a female mannequin in a clothes-shop window. He buys her and in a comic yet disturbing parody of romantic fiction keeps her (it?) in his house, makes love to her, and eventually becomes jealous of her imaginary affair with his chauffeur. In the end, he "murders" her and destroys his own lavish home. "Psychopolis" is set in Los Angeles in the 1970s and recounts the experiences of an English visitor to the city with a group of three articulate and (for him) rather exotic Americans. It is difficult to know how to class the narrator of "Reflections of a Kept Ape." He is, in fact, an ape who is the pet and former lover of a writer suffering a severe creative block. The ape speaks most eloquently of his hopes and dreams for a life with his beloved Sally Klee, but in the end he realizes that he has been rejected forever. It is quite easy to see this piece as a story of a rejected, eternally trapped human lover. The fact that the narrator is an ape makes the story humorous but also emphasizes the hopelessness of the narrator's love.

Those who know McEwan's novels will recognize immediately how they echo subjects, characters, and situations in the short fiction. The incestuous narrator of "Homemade" and the laconic, traumatized twelve-year-old of "Last Day of Summer" anticipate Jack in *The Cement Garden*. The sexual pathology of "Pornography" and "Dead As They Come" is reflected in that of *The Comfort of Strangers*. The father-daughter motifs of "Two Fragments: March 199–" and "In between the Sheets" are obviously central to *The Child in Time*, and the former story's future, apocalyptic setting also anticipates that novel's future dystopia. The contrast and tension between a female emotionalism and a chilly male rationality which is central to "Solid Geometry" is also important in *The Child in Time* and, indeed, in *Black Dogs* and *Enduring Love,* too. The hopeless, obsessed, and pathological lover of "Butterflies," "Reflections of a Kept Ape," and "Dead As They Come" later comes to life in Jed in *Enduring Love*. Clearly, McEwan tries things out in these short stories that he will later develop in the novels.

Each short story is, however, a unique text with its own configuration of narration, narrational technique, language, genre, subject matter, setting, and characters, and each requires and repays close individual analysis. Nevertheless, the stories do exist in the context of their collections, and those two collections do come from a particular period in the author's career and were published close together. It is tempting to see them not only as individual stories, but also as part of a unified group of texts.

THE SHORT STORIES

In fact, the stories in both collections do share a great deal and together build up a relatively coherent picture of the world. Certainly, in terms of narration they have a lot in common. In both collections, first-person narrators dominate. In *First Love, Last Rites*, "Homemade," "Solid Geometry," "Last Day of Summer," "Butterflies," "Conversation with a Cupboard Man," and "First Love, Last Rites" itself are all first-person narrations in which protagonists recount their own stories of crucial experiences in their lives. Among the stories of *In between the Sheets*, the same is true of "Reflections of a Kept Ape," half of "Two Fragments: March 199–," "Dead As They Come," "To and Fro," and "Psychopolis." In the remainder the narration is third-person, but it should be noted that this third-person narration in all but one case operates with a particular character's point of view. This is true in "Disguises" (in *First Love, Last Rites*), in "Pornography" (as far as the aimless, unfeeling O'Byrne has a point of view at all), in the first half of "Two Fragments: March 199–," and in "In between the Sheets" (in *In between the Sheets*). This last story is a little more complex than that, however, inasmuch as the third-person narrator, for the space of just under two pages, shifts from Stephen's point of view to one that is not character based when he moves the setting to Miranda's bedroom and shows things Stephen cannot see. But this shift is very limited within the story, most of which is seen consistently through Stephen's eyes and thoughts.

Narrator's language is also rather homogeneous. Several narrators have a rich, very sophisticated vocabulary and syntax. This is most evident in "Homemade" with its tendency toward lists of adjectives or nouns that build up often into long sentences, marked also by rather formal vocabulary. There are many examples of this language, and the following is representative. The narrator recalls his attitude toward his older male relatives thus: "over our cups of tea I laughed with Raymond at this quiescent betrayal of a lifetime, heaving, digging, shoving, packing, checking, sweating and groaning for the profits of others, at how, to reassure themselves, they made a virtue of this lifetime's grovel, at how they prized themselves for never missing a day in the inferno."[6] Here phrases such as the sophisticated "quiescent betrayal of a lifetime" and the rather unusual and formal "lifetime's grovel" and "prized," the length of the sentence, and the two parallel constructions—the list of participles ("heaving" and so on) and the repeated "at how" structure—give the passage a linguistically elaborate quality (which is appropriate to the wordy, sneering narrator).

There is similar vocabulary and syntax, at least intermittently, in "Reflections of a Kept Ape," "Dead As They Come," and "Psychopolis." In the first, the ape-narrator talks of "scaling drainpipes with uxorious ease," for example.[7] The obsessed businessman in "Dead As They Come" "removed" (not took off) his beloved's boots and lays her in "bed linen" (not sheets), whereupon she falls into a "deep slumber" (instead of sleep) and he "busied" himself (rather than worked) in his library (79). Language takes on a distinctively formal and sophisticated coloration here. In "Psychopolis," too, the narrator's discussion of his flute-playing technique becomes linguistically rather technical and formal (125–26).

Many stories in both volumes, however, are narrated in what is a neutral language, neither very formal nor informal, certainly in terms of vocabulary. This is true of "Cocker at the Theatre," "First Love, Last Rites," "Pornography," "Two Fragments: March 199–," "In between the Sheets," and much of "Psychopolis." Several stories

THE SHORT STORIES

favor a relatively uncomplicated syntax, with a preference for simple and compound sentences. "Last Day of Summer," "Cocker at the Theatre," "Butterflies," "Conversation with a Cupboard Man," and "Pornography" are particularly marked in this respect. The simple sentences that begin "Butterflies" are obviously not the only kind of sentence in these stories, but they do predominate, and they contain a rather informal and unsophisticated vocabulary.

In addition, McEwan aims for local linguistic effects at the informal end of the linguistic spectrum in "First Love, Last Rites," "Disguises," and "Pornography." The first is full of examples of what is technically called parataxis, that is, sentences in which clauses are joined together by coordination rather than subordination. In this story there are many sentences that would be penalized as run-on sentences in a U.S. freshman writing course (among other things, they reflect the fluid, disorganized state of the narrator's emotions in the story). The same technique is very prominent in "Disguises," where the narrator tries to embody Henry's confusion in a sometimes quite extreme syntactic disturbance. For example, in one of the climactic moments of the text, Henry, made drunk, dressed as a girl, and sexually molested, vomits on his aunt. "He rolled off her no longer held, on to the floor with the wig slipping from his head, red and brown stains streaked the fresh white and pink all tawdry now, he pulled the wig clear, 'I'm Henry,' said thickly" (153). Here what should really be four separate sentences is fused together with nothing but commas, and the personal pronoun in the last clause is lacking. Punctuation and syntax are strikingly and effectively deviant in this story. In "Pornography," too, informal syntax is used to achieve a particular effect. The fragments in the first few pages of the story are intended to capture the static aimlessness of O'Byrne's present life. See, for example, the second sentence of the story, or the way O'Byrne's slow, lizardlike gaze is represented by his registering of his brother's clothes ("Harold's new leather jacket" [13]).

Linguistically, at first glance "To and Fro" stands out from the other stories (its page layout is also unusual). It does so because it appears to be aiming to be a kind of prose poem, to achieve an incantation-like effect by repeating words and phrases, such as the "to and fro" in the title. It also has a much greater frequency of metaphor than the other stories. However, many of the features of the story's language are evident in those other stories. A quite sophisticated vocabulary and syntax and a fondness for lists and other parallel structures are familiar from a radically different story such as "Homemade." For instance, note the formal vocabulary ("assume a shape inclusive of the optical limits of sight"), sentence length, use of metaphor ("black-furred sleep," "patient heroism of being awake," "ancient, soft to and fro," "the Arctic hole"), and parallelism ("I lie in the dark and look in, I lie in it and gaze out") on pages 114–15 of "To and Fro," and compare them to the equally formal and sophisticated language of the quite different speaker in "Homemade."

"To and Fro" also differs from the other stories in both collections because its narrative element is very limited. It barely tells a story or recounts events at all. There are certainly some occurrences (although of a very ambiguous nature—is Leech really a separate character, or the narrator's alter ego?), mostly in the office parts of the text. The bed parts are evocations of mood, descriptions of the loved one, memories of impressions (indeed, the whole text is really not a narrative at all, but a piece of lyric expression). "To and Fro"

THE SHORT STORIES

is also unusual among McEwan's stories because the narrative organization is more complex than in the remainder of them. The story moves backward and forward between two times and places in a regular, but far from linear, fashion. This is appropriate to the text's attempt to express mood and emotion, but is quite untypical of McEwan's stories. All the other stories in both volumes are linear narratives that follow a clear logical-chronological sequence. Where there are retrospects, these are clearly marked. "Homemade" and "Pornography," "Butterflies" and "Psychopolis" all tell their stories in a clear, traditional manner, observing sequence in terms of time and cause and effect. There is no narrative experimentation in these stories, just as there is none in terms of narration. There is no radical breaking of logic and chronology, no unreliable narrators (McEwan's narrators are not pleasant characters sometimes, but they are painfully honest), no questions raised about how narratives are made and transmitted. There is very little of the experimentation of early- twentieth-century or late-twentieth-century European and North American literature. If readers were shocked, this had nothing to do with deviations from mainstream nineteenth- and twentieth-century, rather conservative technique.

In terms of genre the stories in *First Love, Last Rites* and *In between the Sheets* also show a considerable degree of homogeneity and, indeed, traditionality. They are almost all psychological pieces, the central focus of which is on a character's mental and emotional make-up and/or development. This is clearly true of all the stories in *First Love, Last Rites* except "Cocker at the Theatre," which is very hard to place in terms of genre, but is some kind of social and moral satire. The rest, however, are rather detailed and painstaking evocations of mood and feeling, of desire, shame, uncertainty, distaste, and confusion. The same is true of the texts in *In between the Sheets*. The revealingly titled "Psychopolis" (psychological city, city of psychological, even psychologically disturbed, states), "To and Fro," "In between the Sheets," "Dead As They Come" (the confession of a psychopath, no less), and "Reflections of a Kept Ape" (with its focus on the disappointed ape-lover's despair, and the writer's inertia)—all these are examples of the psychological focus of McEwan's fiction at this stage. Even the dystopic "Two Fragments: March 199–" really concentrates on the protagonist's relationship with his daughter and his former lover, and the desolation of his surroundings becomes a metaphor for his inertia and despair. It is, in a way, hard to talk about "Pornography" as a psychological piece because the unsavory O'Byrne lacks the consciousness of self, and any kind of emotional life or even thought, which would permit a psychological study. Yet even in this story O'Byrne's growing realization that he likes being dominated by the forceful and demanding Lucy, and his erection as the women prepare to mutilate him, indicate that, in the end, the text does have a psychological focus.

As regards genre, "Pornography" is also complex, because there is a hint of the horror story in the revenge the nurses prepare for the protagonist, and also because it is, like "Dead As They Come," very near to the kind of rape and bondage fantasies that are a staple of pornographic publications. (Pornography is, of course, not a genre, but it is a class of text, and one that some of McEwan's stories refer to.) Two of McEwan's other stories contain elements not drawn from traditional psychological narratives. One of these is "Solid Geometry," in which the protagonist-narrator's hostility toward his wife culminates in his making her disappear by a revolutionary piece of mathematical-geometric manipulation. This act is surrounded by details that aim to make the whole thing sound probable, such as the account of the mathematical convention at which the revolution in geometry is announced, the pages of proofs that are alluded to, and the technical vocabulary that the narrator employs. These are elements that are drawn from science fiction, and they do add another aspect of genre to what is still a text primarily about a broken marriage and hostility between men and women.

"Reflections of a Kept Ape," with its eloquent simian narrator, clearly alludes to the traditional genre of the beast fable, in which animals embody human qualities and have the ability to speak. But once again, the psychological purpose (capturing the ape's despair) of the text dominates. One of the most striking aspects of genre in the two collections of stories is how little genre mixture there is. Almost certainly, the length of the short story means that there are fewer opportunities for genre mixing (and less reason for it) than in the novel, but McEwan's later fiction, especially *The Child in Time* and *The Innocent* and, to a lesser extent, *The Cement Garden* and *The Comfort of Strangers*, is mixed in terms of genre. In the volumes of short stories, both individual texts are fairly pure as far as genre goes, and the collections as wholes are rooted in the well-established tradition (in terms of British literary history) of psychological fiction.

Both *First Love, Last Rites* and *In between the Sheets* are collections of very traditional, rather conservative stories. This is so in terms of the kind of events they depict, the characters involved, the issues generated by the relationships of those characters, the stories' settings, and certain images that run throughout them. Even the metafictional elements that some stories have can be seen to be at least fashionable, if not, by the late 1970s, somewhat traditional.

First, the kind of events depicted in the stories is traditional. In a 1979 interview with Christopher Ricks, McEwan, discussing his interest in adolescents, argues that they fascinate him because they are close to childhood and yet are constantly "baffled and irritated by the initiations into what's on the other side—the shadow line, as it were."[8] This comment is revealing on two connected accounts. It suggests the nature of many of the central events depicted in McEwan's short fiction, and it also, by the allusion to Joseph Conrad's famous short story "The Shadow-Line" (1917), indicates the literary tradition within which he is operating. Most of the stories in *First Love, Last Rites* can be described as stories of initiation. If the initiation is obscure in the title story (what do the narrator and his girlfriend learn from the dead rat's pregnant body?), it is certainly there, as it is in the narrator's first experience of sexual intercourse in "Homemade," in the narrator's first sexual experience in "Butterflies," in Henry's induction into the confused world of adult games and sexuality, and also in childhood friendship in "Disguises." Even "Last Day of Summer" depicts a further initiation for the protagonist-narrator into the world of sadness and loss. Of all the stories in this volume, only "Solid Geometry," "Cocker at the Theatre," and "Conversation with a Cupboard Man" do not show initiations of some sort.

The stories of *In between the Sheets* do not show initiations, but they do present the related experience of revelation, of epiphany (and the use of the Joycean term here suggests how these stories, too, are within an enduring and durable tradition of the short story). "In between the Sheets" shows the protagonist's realization that his daughter is just a young girl, and he has, in a moment of insight, a sense of the innocence that his adult life has muddied. The ape in

THE SHORT STORIES

"Reflections of a Kept Ape" realizes that he will never possess Sally Klee and that both he and she are trapped forever. In "Pornography" O'Byrne's mutilation is also a moment of epiphany, and at the end of "Psychopolis" the narrator, too, has come to a sense of the glorious fragmentation and diffuseness of life in Los Angeles, against which his badly played Bach sonata sounds old-fashioned, alien, and inane. One might even argue that the reader (if not the narrator) is meant to realize the futile inertia of life (for example, the human contact with the Chinese family leads to absolutely nothing) at the conclusion of the two parts of "Two Fragments: March 199–." "Dead As They Come" and "To and Fro" present neither initiation nor epiphany. The former shows the working out of an obsession on the part of a character quite without insight into himself or others, while the latter evokes an essentially static state that does not allow for the movement or change necessary for revelation or transition. But the majority of the stories in this volume depict something like an initiation, a moment of realization that is the stuff of dozens of twentieth-century short stories.

Another traditional feature of McEwan's short stories is the way in which narrators and characters are the alienated, the losers, the isolated and marginalized figures that are a central focus of much English-language twentieth-century fiction in general (as well as of short fiction).[9] Such figures are certainly prominent in McEwan's short stories—psychopaths and sociopaths, the stranger and the rule-breaker. For example, the narrator of "Homemade" is a serial masturbator, underage smoker and drinker, shoplifter, derider of his elders, and guilty of incest. He celebrates, too, the losers, the failures in school sports (19–20). In "Cocker at the Theater," the two actors who make love break the rules of a theatrical performance in which only simulation is allowed. They are expelled from the company. The narrator of "Reflections of a Kept Ape" is an ape in a human world, a species outsider; that of "Psychopolis" is the ultimate alien, an Englishman in Los Angeles. There are many other examples. The boy in "Last Day of Summer" is a child in an adult world, as is Henry in "Disguises," while the narrator in "Conversation with a Cupboard Man" is a deeply alienated figure who finally feels happy only when he is locked up in a cupboard. Even the young couple in "First Love, Last Rites" is strangely isolated in the town where they live, and has little contact with those who live and work there too.

Indeed, although some of the characters in McEwan's short stories are connected with society, politics, and history, many seem to lead lives that have at best tangential connections with larger, impersonal forces beyond their families, their rooms, and their lovers. Even if the way they make their living is sometimes scarcely the way of most people, the stories do show how Sissel ("First Love, Last Rites"), O'Byrne ("Pornography"), the protagonist of "Two Fragments: March 199–," the narrator of "To and Fro," and the businessman-lover in "Dead As They Come" earn money. But even with these characters, the emphasis in their lives mostly falls elsewhere, in all the above cases in bed. In other stories, many characters are somehow divorced from society and history, free to pursue their own isolated, alienated, and alienating obsessions. School has not yet taken the narrator of "Last Day of Summer"; the cupboard man has tried the world of work, but now retreats from it into his closet ("Conversation with a Cupboard Man"); the narrator of "Solid Geometry" has the freedom from social constraints to sit at a desk and do little but read his great-grandfather's diaries; Henry's aunt's house in "Disguises" is largely a place apart from the rest of society. One has a sense of enclosed worlds in which characters live cut off often from others, with few visitors and few contacts with work, police, or school.

However, one point of contact between the characters of these stories and a wider social world is in the field of gender and of gender roles and relations. (Here, too, the traditionality of McEwan's stories is evident. Surely such roles and relations form one of the great concerns of much twentieth-century fiction and, indeed, of literature in general.) This focus on the complexity of gender runs throughout McEwan's later fiction and is very evident in the short stories. They present a complex picture of male-female relations and gender roles. In "Psychopolis" Mary both acts out a fantasy of being dominated by a male and puts forward an explicitly feminist argument about religion. The stories show male characters learning to act as traditional males to try to dominate and, indeed, abuse female figures. "Homemade" and "Butterflies" illustrate this most vividly, while the implications and absurdities of this kind of male role are the subject of "Dead As They Come" (the most convenient kind of woman is an object, a store mannequin, although even she fights back in odd ways). "Pornography" also suggests the brutalities and complexities of the traditional male exploiter of women, and "Solid Geometry" is a study of bitter, chilly misogyny and its logical consequences. Yet McEwan also shows less-disturbed relations between male and female: the complex ebb and flow of feelings in "First Love, Last Rites," the redemptive realization of innocence in "In between the Sheets," and the rich, saving warmth of "To and Fro" (although one should note that the girl and women characters in all these stories follow very traditional female roles: inscrutable fertility [Sissel], innocent seductress [Miranda], and earth mother in bed [the woman in "To and Fro"]).

If men are often shown as brutal violators and controllers of women, female characters, too, have a streak of nastiness in them: the mother who infantilizes the cupboard man and then abandons him, Mina who draws her nephew into her sexual fantasies ("Disguises"), Sally Klee who takes up and then abandons her adoring ape. Further, although the female figure in "To and Fro" is the source of all that is valuable and wondrous in the world of that short story, the ladies in "Pornography" who are about to excise O'Byrne's penis are altogether of a different mettle (this is surely resistance to the oppressor!).

Certain recurrent settings and images also place McEwan's short stories foursquare in a long twentieth-century tradition. His characters move through the drab wasteland of so much literature of the past century, trapped in the entropic world that is part of the twentieth-century vision of things. The narrator of "Homemade" loves to wait for the lagging runners in a school race "in that vast dismal field, surrounded on all sides by factories, pylons, dull houses and garages, a cold wind rising, bringing the beginnings of a bitter drizzle, waiting there in that heavy gloom" (20). The narrator in "Butterflies" leads his victim to her death by a reeking canal, past disused lots, abandoned scrap yards, and empty factories (89–93). "Pornography" is set in rainy Soho streets, a "dank, deserted" pub, anonymous flats, and a pornographic magazine warehouse in "a disused church in a narrow terraced street on the Brixton side of Norbury" (a drab South London suburb) (12, 14, 19). The postapocalyptic, urban wasteland of "Two Fragments: March 199–" seems only a heightening of the dismal settings of the contemporary stories.

In this landscape, characters are constantly seen as entrapped in some way. In four of the stories there are references to animals that have been cruelly roasted alive ("Homemade," "Butterflies," "Conversation with a Cupboard Man," and "Two Fragments: March 199–"). This recurrent reference captures the painful trap in which many characters find or place themselves. The narrator's and his girlfriend's immobility in "First Love, Last Rites" is reflected in the eel traps he is making; the cupboard man is confined by his mother, shut up in an oven (twice) by his enemy, locked up in jail for shoplifting, and finally chooses his own prison in the closet ("Conversation with a Cupboard Man"). The protagonists of "Two Fragments: March 199–" can never leave the decaying city; Mary in "Psychopolis" has the narrator tie her up; and O'Byrne ends up strapped to a bed while his girlfriends prepare to cut off his penis.

Where characters are not confined, they frequently live in indecisive, inert, and entropic circumstances. The narrator in "Last Day of Summer" sometimes feels no impulse to do anything, one thing rather than another (68), a situation that the narrator of "Butterflies" shares. "I walked off to the left," he says, "because that was the way I was facing" (80). The cupboard man likes jail because he does not have to make decisions, change, or do anything very much at all. "If they had made us stay in them [our cells] all day I don't think I would have complained" (112). At first, Henry (in "Disguises") dresses up for his aunt without asking questions or caring much—he "was uncurious, obedient, put on each evening what he found at the foot of his bed" (136). The two lovers in "First Love, Last Rites" start to live in a simultaneously inert and decaying world. "Sissel grew tired of her records, and her foot rot spread from one foot to the other and added to the smell. Our room stank. . . . We made love less and our rubbish gathered around us, milk bottles we could not bring ourselves to carry away, grey sweating cheese, butter wrappers, yogurt cartons, over-ripe salami"(121–22). The exposed fetal rats toward the story's end are not quite dead yet, but cannot live—"One unborn rat quivered as if in hope, but the mother was hopelessly dead and there was no more for it" (128).

Things are scarcely more vibrant in *In between the Sheets*. Sally Klee will never write another novel; the ape will never be her lover again. Indeed, at the end they both are frozen in postures that will never change. "Now I am here, it seems impossible she will ever turn in her chair and notice me," the narrator concludes sadly (48). The principal characters of "In between the Sheets" and "Psychopolis" also are at times held in an apathetic stasis. For example, note the narrator's description of a torpid day in Los Angeles (135–37). In "Two Fragments: March 199–" the crumbling city with its windswept empty spaces and drying River Thames reflects the main character's own mental and spiritual deadness, while O'Byrne in "Pornography" is a hollow man moving listlessly, unreflectingly through the world. See, for example, the painstaking description of his aimless actions while waiting for Pauline (15–17). The obsessive businessman of "Dead As They Come" is almost a relief; at least he cares about something.

McEwan's stories are powerful evocations of a wasteland, of entrapment, and of aimless inertia. But these settings and these repeated images are the stuff of twentieth-century literature in English, including short fiction. They are not, of course, by any means the only settings or recurrent images in twentieth-century short fiction in English, but they are very common ones. The detailed evocations of hopeless paralysis, spiritual emptiness, and decay that run throughout twentieth-century fiction are surely echoed in McEwan's studies of accidie and atrophy.

The critic in the *New York Times Book Review*, who dislikes *In between the Sheets* fairly thoroughly, sees this volume's stories' "advanced modern manner" as "owing something to Nabokov and Beckett."[10] McEwan himself has said that he was imitating particular experimental writers' work in his early short fiction.[11] There are certainly some metafictional elements (in the "advanced modern manner") in the two collections, that is, aspects of a story that emphasize it is a text, and a literary text at that, and ones that also touch upon problems and possibilities of writing fiction. "Homemade," for example, is a very allusive text, with references to Spenser (11), Dante (13), the Faust material (13), Coleridge's "The Rhyme of the Ancient Mariner" (15), Havelock Ellis and Henry Miller (16), the search for the Holy Grail (18), existentialism (19), Shakespeare (20), and Jane Austen (22). This goes beyond the establishing of a particular narrator's character, and also draws the reader's attention to the story as literary text, as a work of fiction. "Dead As They Come," too, reads at times like a conscious parody of contemporary romantic fiction, or at least its pornographic variant (80). "To and Fro" is a clearly self-consciously poetic piece in which repetitions, parallelisms, and a frequency of metaphor make the text itself the object of the reader's attention, much of the time drawing attention away from the objects, characters, or experiences referred to. "Reflections of a Kept Ape" has, on the other hand, a writer and her block, her hopeless inertia, as one of its main subjects.

All this is interesting and important (for McEwan's later work and in terms of the development of late-twentieth-century British fiction), but it is not enormously innovative. Indeed, at this stage in his career, McEwan is actually rather modest in the amount of metafictional material he includes in his short stories. There is much more of it in the novels in the following two decades. Once again, one can see McEwan working well within the traditional limits of contemporary fiction.

But, for all that, these are shocking stories.[12] And the shocking element lies surely in their subject matter. The recurrent references to taboo subjects are meant to disturb the reader; the closeness of what is being presented as serious, mainstream literature to pornography is intended to upset. "Homemade" painstakingly recounts feats of masturbation and incest. In "Solid Geometry" a pickled penis in a jar is a prominent image. A couple makes love in public in "Cocker at the Theatre." "Butterflies" recounts the sexual molestation of a young girl and her murder. There are many other examples. Bodily fluids, excrement, genitalia, unsavory odors, a disemboweled rat, transvestite sex with a minor, fetishism, incest—the stories abound and drip with them. It is all quite strong stuff, even for the most blasé of readers (although not completely new to readers of D. H. Lawrence, Joyce, Henry Miller, William Burroughs, or even John Fowles). But perhaps what is really disturbing in these stories are two crucial aspects of the way McEwan presents his subject matter: the particular perspective that he persistently adopts toward human life, and the question of moral judgment in them.

In both *First Love, Last Rites* and, to a lesser extent, *In between the Sheets*, familiar human actions and emotions (bringing up children, falling in love, social contacts with other humans) are seen from an oblique and uncomprehending point of view. This serves to make them unfamiliar and strange, and invites the reader to consider what is normally taken for granted. In the *Partisan Review*, Neil Schmitz writes that McEwan's stories present "the strange, in a hard light."[13] But rather than that, it seems that McEwan often aims to make the familiar strange. Cowley notes that McEwan believes that the aim of the artist (and the scientist) is to "'deanesthetise the familiar'—by which he means that the world around us, the world to which we have come to consciousness from babyhood, has a wonder with which we have become too familiar."[14] This aim—of defamiliarizing what readers take for granted—is one that the noted Russian Formalist scholar Viktor Shklovsky sees as central to much art. "Habitualization," he argues in one passage, "devours works, clothes, furniture, one's wife, and the fear of war."[15] It is the purpose of art, he goes on, to destroy this fatal automatization, this deadening of perception, to help the reader to see things afresh.

In *First Love, Last Rites*, the familiar is constantly defamiliarized by an alien, often uncomprehending point of view. In "Homemade" it is supplied by Connie, the narrator's ten-year-old sister, and her incredulous perspective on sexual intercourse (26, 28). What is usually taken for granted is suddenly seen again in a fresh light, as it is in the context of lust and sexual abuse in "Butterflies." The young narrator of "Last Day of Summer" also casts a slightly uncomprehending eye on adult behavior and social conventions. At one point he muses that "we're just animals with clothes on doing very peculiar things like monkeys at a tea party. But we get so used to each other most of the time" (64). The remainder of the stories in the collection also see familiar human acts as "very peculiar things"—the conventions of simulating sex on stage, for example

("Cocker at the Theatre"), or even human intimacy (through the eyes of Sissel's brother in "First Love, Last Rites" [121]). "Conversation with a Cupboard Man" invites us to look again at the way children are treated (98) and concludes with a strongly defamiliarizing vision of traditional notions of the benefits of growing up and of the sense of everyday adult activities (113).

"Disguises" defamiliarizes various aspects of adult sexuality—in the transvestite games that Mina plays, but also in Henry's and Linda's view of Linda's mother's lover (148)—and also other conventions of adult social behavior in Henry's observation of what goes on at his aunt's party (162–63). *In between the Sheets*, similarly, deautomatizes the reader's perception of common human actions. To have an ape fall in love and look uncomprehendingly at the way humans treat their lovers, and also to have the sympathetic ape talk about the ways in which he dreams of fitting into human society, both satirizes and strips a layer of familiarity off human behavior (37–38). And, of course, "Dead As They Come" is a biting exposure of traditional male attitudes toward women. The best woman is a store-window dummy; when she dies she is really having pleasure; the man knows best what she likes and wants. "I know her death was a moment of intense pleasure to her. I heard her shouts through the pillows," the narrator assures the reader (92). Viewing male-female relations through the eyes of an obsessional psychopath defamiliarizes them and also, to one's discomfort, echoes traditional and widespread attitudes.

All this is disturbing enough, but perhaps the most shocking aspect of McEwan's short stories is, paradoxically, their lack of moral judgment. Jack Slay, Jr., attempts manfully to persuade his readers that McEwan's exposures of cruel behavior are suggestions that they try to reform themselves and the world.[16] This is not true, however. Kiernan Ryan argues the opposite, at least with regard to *First Love, Last Rites*. "What makes such narratives hard to swallow," he writes, "is not so much the author's soft spot for the gruesome as his seeming content to withhold moral appraisal, to let the monstrous smuggle itself out of his unconscious duty-free."[17] The issue is quite complex. The presentation of male sexuality in "Homemade" or in "Dead As They Come" certainly serves to defamilarize traditional ways of behaving and thinking. But there seems very little overt disapproval of characters and actions. The narrator of "Butterflies" is a child-molester and murderer, but it is the reader who brings moral attitudes to the story, for they are absent in the text itself. The same is true of the depictions of what is usually classed as perverse sexual activities in "Disguises" and "Pornography." It is hard to see where the narrator's moral disapproval (or approval) falls. "Two Fragments: March 199–" and "Psychopolis" are notably without any moral commentary at all, and even with "In between the Sheets" the reader cannot be sure that Stephen's original perception of his daughter's sexuality is entirely wrong. Only "To and Fro" has a clear moral vision: that the warm, rich world of bed is better than the dull, sterile world of work. Of all the stories, this one alone confirms Slay's argument that McEwan is suggesting the importance and possibilities of rich and rewarding human relationships.[18]

And yet, there are hints of moral attitudes in some stories. The male copulator walks off unbowed in "Cocker at the Theatre"; "First Love, Last Rites" concludes with Sissel's warm belly and a very positive-sounding "Yes" that suggests some kind of future development; similarly, "In between the Sheets" finishes with Stephen's vision of his daughter's innocence as "a field of dazzling white snow"

(112). These invite certain moral responses from the reader. But they are at most hints, and finally one is faced with the fact that many stories in both volumes lack any moral center at all. This makes them the uncomfortable texts that they are. It also points toward the equally disturbing lack of moral focus in McEwan's first novel, *The Cement Garden.*

Fiction and Evil (I)
The Cement Garden

Critics tend to view *The Cement Garden* (1978) with a mixture of fascination and slight horror. "*Ein unerbaulicher Roman*" (an unedifying novel), remarks Wolfgang Wicht; Jack is "*ce monstre d' insensibilité*" (this unfeeling monster), notes Gérard Klaus. Reviews constantly, and rightly, point to the macabre aspects of the novel's action but also find it a striking achievement. "*The Cement Garden* is in many ways a shocking book," writes Robert Towers in the *New York Review of Books*, "morbid, full of repellent imagery—and irresistibly readable." Despite his disapproval of what he describes as its typically British agoraphobic qualities, Paul Abelman in the *Spectator* describes the novel as "just about perfect," and in the *Times Literary Supplement*, Blake Morrison suggests that "it should consolidate Ian McEwan's reputation as one of the best young writers in Britain today."[1]

The story told by *The Cement Garden* is certainly unsavory. The adolescent Jack tells of his unloved and unlovable father's death at the beginning of a manic attempt to concrete over the family garden. Jack goes on to describe his mother's slow demise from an unspecified wasting disease. On her death, Jack and his two sisters and brother, fearing that they will be parted, decide to bury her body in a metal trunk filled with concrete in the cellar. The novel then proceeds to chart the actions of the children in their freedom from any parental and social authority. This freedom has, in any case, existed since the mother took to her bed, but now it assumes quite extreme forms. Jack spends entire days sleeping and masturbating; his younger sister Sue withdraws into her novels and her diary; she and her elder sister Julie dress the younger brother Tom in girl's clothes, and Tom not only willingly wears these, but at other times regresses into babyhood; they all allow the house to fill with decaying refuse. In the cellar the ill-made concrete tomb starts to crack and the odor of the mother's decomposing corpse fills the house. The novel's climax comes when Julie's boyfriend, Derek, smashes open the trunk while Julie and Jack have sexual intercourse upstairs next to the sleeping Tom. The novel concludes with the children awaiting the arrival of the police.

The novel is narrated by the fifteen-year-old Jack, a protagonist himself deeply involved in the novel's action. The narration is, however, far from straightforward. Wicht has pointed out how the narrational strategy of McEwan's novel diverges from that of the classic, realist "I" narrator of Dickens's *David Copperfield*. The two narrators differ in the clear morals and values embodied and expressed by Dickens's David, as opposed to the utter lack of such in McEwan's Jack. But they also differ in the way in which the implied author of the text conceals his existence in Dickens's novel, integrates his perspective entirely with that of his protagonist-narrator, and fosters the reader's self-identification with and trust in that figure. In the McEwan novel, Wicht argues, one is encouraged to distrust the narrator (by, among other devices, the extreme emphasis on "I" in the opening paragraph of the text), and also to see Jack as a function of the implied author's purposes in the text rather than as a mimetic representation.[2] Despite the obscurities of Wicht's article, he points to some real complexities in the figure of the narrator in *The Cement Garden*.

FICTION AND EVIL (I)

In one sense, Jack performs the traditional function of a first-person narrator by taking the reader into a hidden world and looking at it from a particular point of view. But although he is narrating his own story, Jack's point of view is often not participatory at all, but rather exterior and detached. The two paragraphs in chapter 1 in which Jack ejaculates for the first time and in which his father dies are representative of this peculiar quality in the narration.[3] These paragraphs set forth extreme and important occurrences, a sexual initiation and the death of a father. The vocabulary, however, is abstract and impersonal—"boredom and familiar longings were slowing my movements," "the image before me was." Even where the narrator plays the grammatical role of agent, language is still clinical and uninvolved—"I worked on myself rapidly," "now I was astonished and moved." There are many ways of representing, as opposed to recounting, astonishment and strong emotion; these words are not one of them. The entire passage is utterly devoid of any but the most abstractly expressed feeling; externalities, not emotions, are observed and recorded. The reader knows that Jack "yawned frequently" and that he puts his hands inside his underpants, but not what he feels. This is emphasized by those phrases that tell the reader in rudimentary fashion what he is thinking: "I wondered where my sisters were. Why weren't they helping?" and "I remembered my father waiting." The paragraph in which Jack discovers his father's body lying by the wet concrete is even more marked by its restriction to the externally observable. The only occasions on which one sees his thought processes provide very superficial information. Jack approaches the body, "knowing I had to run for help"; he does not "have a thought" in his head as he smooths away the marks of his father's body in the wet concrete. Jack spends much more space describing his seminal fluid or the physical appearance and position of his father's corpse. The first-person narration is marked by absence of revealed emotion, of motivation (why does Jack wait before he tells anyone?), and of the opportunity for self-identification of reader with narrator. These are all antitheses of the traditional purposes of such a narrative technique.

In the course of the text, one comes to see Jack as an unreliable narrator. His evasions are not always clearly marked, but, already indicated in the strangely detached focus of the narration, they are emphasized in one passage where Jack is confronted with another's view of events, that of his sister Sue. In her diary, which she reads to him, she records some matters that the reader knows well from Jack's account—for example, his physical appearance. She, however, also records his violence toward the others in the house, a violence of which Jack has said little. She also notes that his surprise and anger when Julie, according to him, first mentions Derek and then brings him home are dishonest (89–90, 98–104). "Julie talked about her bloke who is called Derek," Sue reads. "She said she might bring him home one time and did we mind. I said no. Jack pretended he didn't hear and went upstairs" (109). Jack continues to deny this conversation took place, but one is certainly being further encouraged to distrust him.

Indeed, motifs of memory, of forgetting, and of false memory recur throughout the text, all serving to reinforce a distrust of Jack as a narrator. The children's house is described by Jack as looking "like the face of someone concentrating, trying to remember" (28). Some time later, while looking at his mother's tomb in the cellar, he reflects that "it was not at all clear to me now why we had put her in the trunk in the first place" (98). Sue claims she hardly remembers the game of sexual exploration she played with Jack and Julie (106–7); Jack denies Sue's memories of being "horrible" to his mother (108); the children disagree about how often it has rained since their mother died (122). Julie and Jack try to persuade Tom to "remember" Jack's dog Cosmo, supposedly buried in the trunk downstairs, for the benefit of the suspicious Derek (140). Toward the novel's end Julie confesses that she cannot "remember how it used to be when Mum was alive" (149).

One's sense of something not quite right with regard to the narration is augmented (as it is in the novels of some of McEwan's contemporaries, such as Graham Swift and Kazuo Ishiguro) when one considers stylistic aspects of Jack's voice. This voice has received attention from critics, Abelman calling it "spare, rather grey prose" and Anthony Thwaite describing it as "laconically efficient."[4] In some respects Jack speaks what is almost a British Hemingwayesque. See, for example, his lines on his father's ornamental garden (19). Simple sentences and an informal, everyday vocabulary predominate in this passage. But even within such a passage, there seem slight slippages from the predominant style. Such phrases as "He alone," "He would have nothing that tangled," and "In summer the vacant sites grew lush with weeds" seem to belong to a more literary and educated style than the one the reader might expect from Jack.

A passage a few pages later in the novel, in which Jack examines himself in a mirror, confirms this impression of stylistic oscillation (26–27). Here a quintessential and complicated adolescent experience is rendered in a style that is itself an intricate mixture of the simple and the complex. Note the dominant simple sentences and the vulgarity of the words in quotation marks. But note, too, that the loutish Jack expresses himself through a very sophisticated vocabulary. This is apparent from the slightly formal "had always intended to secure it" and "illuminated from behind," to "obscured the humps and pits of my complexion" and "began to dissociate itself and paralyse me with its look." The paragraph ends with the highly formal "in weary admonition." This is not the language one normally associates with pubescent fifteen-year-old boys, especially those who are poor scholars and readers such as the reader knows Jack to be. (He reads only one book in the course of the text, the first he has ever "read all the way through" [43], and the story of Commander Hunt scarcely seems the kind of novel where one would find such phrases as "weary admonition.")

Such a peculiar narrational strategy seems to have several functions in the text. First, the narrator's emotional reserve contributes to the reader's sense of the utterly desolate and dead world which the characters inhabit, a world represented, among much else, by the father's plan to concrete over the garden around the house. Second, in its refusal to allow emotional self-identification with the narrator, the novel stakes out a very rigorous and consequential moral position vis-à-vis its world and characters. It denies its readers any large measure of sentimental empathy with its characters. One does not forgive Jack and his brother and sisters because one is able to see into their souls and feelings. In fact, they do not ask for forgiveness or understanding (in a sentimental sense) at all, for the novel would deny that there is any firm moral ground from which to judge and forgive them. They are what they are and they do what they do, and the novel refuses to make any kind of special plea on their behalf. Third, stylistic aspects of the narrator's voice foster this alienation of the reader, making one uneasy, repelling sympathy, just as the detailed depictions of the physically unpleasant do. Also, finally, the intricate slippage from stylistic level to stylistic level, so that it becomes extremely hard to accept Jack's voice as that of the kind of fifteen-year-old boy he tells us he is, can be seen as a self-referential device, advertising the figure of the implied author behind all the verisimilar details of the text and emphasizing that the characters are not people but only simulacra, functional units in the overall scheme of the text. Narration makes a metafictional point among many others.

Just as the narrator's voice is marked by stylistic slippages, so, too, does the text as a whole move between at least two genres. McEwan's first novel, preceding as it does the novels of many writers of his generation who come to prominence in the 1980s, points the way to the genre mixing which is so much a part of British fiction of that decade. On one level, *The Cement Garden* is a psychological study of adolescence. Centered on the narrator, it charts family relationships and tensions: between father and son, between mother and children, and among siblings. Jack's Oedipal hostility toward his father, expressed so tellingly when they are moving bags of cement ("I made sure he took as much weight as I did" [18]), exemplifies this aspect of the text, as does Julie and Jack's game with the naked Sue (15–16). Psychological tensions, conflicts, longings, and rejections abound in the text. A particularly striking example of this level of the text occurs when Jack, feeling guilty about his behavior toward his mother, returns home, observes her closely, yet runs away when she calls to him (31–32). Here the narrator's fascination with, affection for, and rejection of his mother are memorably expressed. The novel as a whole moves toward a climactic moment of initiation which is so much part of the pattern of such psychological texts, charting as they often do the passage from adolescence to maturity. In *The Cement Garden* such a moment is Jack and Julie's coming together in sexual intercourse (146–52). But here the initiation is scarcely a traditional one and can only with difficulty be described as marking a passage to maturity. Indeed, the whole episode, which starts off with naked Jack lying next to naked Tom in the latter's cot, seems much more a kind of regression. "Two bare babies!" exclaims Julie when she sees them (146). The moment of initiation seems an ironic reversal of generic expectations.

The Cement Garden is also marked by the clear presence of gothic elements. The family house with its dark cellar that comes to hold a grisly secret is a typical gothic or neogothic setting (there are echoes of both Poe's "The Fall of the House of Usher" and Hitchcock's *Psycho* here). But several local details point toward this genre. The men who deliver the cement "were covered in a fine, pale dust which gave their faces a ghostly look" (13). Jack's nightmare of the box with a small, captive, stinking creature inside it (23) and his tormenting Julie with his father's "enormous" gardening gloves (36–37) also set up gothic echoes. But these are most clear when the children bury their mother in the cement-filled trunk in the basement and when, after a few weeks, the smell of her decomposing body starts to drift through the house (130–31).

The novel also echoes certain specific texts. It clearly refers back to that other British adolescent dystopia, William Golding's *Lord of the Flies* (1954), although the utter lack of any moral norms or expression of traditional morality in the text differentiates McEwan's novel from Golding's. The everyday, domestic setting of the later novel also distances it from the earlier one with its exotic, desert island location, perhaps making McEwan's text all the more frightening in its depiction of the collapse of traditional rules and order. A further intertextual echo is of the plays of Harold Pinter, especially of a piece like *The Homecoming* (1965). The desolate, modern London setting, the brutal and incestuous family tensions, the world of the snooker hall, and Derek's prying, menacing questions (113–20) all echo Pinter.

Genre mixture in *The Cement Garden* has a quite different function from that which it has in the novels of several of McEwan's contemporaries. The effect of genre mixture in the novels of these authors (for example, Graham Swift's *Waterland* [1983]) is to raise metaliterary points about the possibility of giving reliable accounts of events. In *The Cement Garden* the function of such mixing is rather to suggest, in true Pinteresque fashion, the potential for the seemingly normal, banal, and everyday to tip into the grim and macabre. The gothic intrudes on the psychological narrative, just as bizarre death, mother burial, transvestism, infantile regression, and incest penetrate the seemingly normal world of the family. Aspects of genre within the text as well as intertextual reference, however, do have some metaliterary points to make. Both allow McEwan to express distrust of traditional maturation narratives and of childhood dystopias. The initiation story, repeated ad nauseam in twentieth-century short stories and novels, is cruelly twisted in *The Cement Garden*. It is exposed as false, just like traditional notions of normality and family, which the novel also shows to be faulty. In addition, the setting of the story in contemporary Britain passes comment on narratives like *Lord of the Flies* that choose exotic settings to expose a barbarism in human life. For McEwan the heart of darkness is fully here and now, and needs no distant, savage locale to bring it forth.

Time, place, and character are at once specific and general in

The Cement Garden. The novel obviously takes place in a fairly contemporary Britain. The urban desolation that surrounds the family home in the novel indicates this. However, even here there are peculiar features: there is no television in Jack's house; his narrative lacks the kind of specific reference to adolescent culture that would allow one to date the story precisely; Julie's "starched white petticoats" (25) would place the novel's setting some fifteen or more years before its publication. In fact, the text seems to be avoiding the kind of local temporal color that would allow one to pin down its setting, clearly aiming for a generality of reference.

Such references to time as there are in the novel involve Jack's quite solipsistic, internal frame of reference. They take the form of phrases such as "in the early summer of my fourteenth year" (13), "during the following year" (25), "shortly before my fifteenth birthday" (26), and "three days later" (59) or "three weeks after Mother died" (91). It is as if Jack has lost any connection with any established, external scheme of things (just as traditional moral standards seem to have no meaning for him). The only such points of reference come when his mother dies "on Friday afternoon, the last day of the summer term" (59), and when Julie and Jack almost at the novel's end decide not to go back to school when it starts again "next week" (148). Indeed, the novel's action seems strangely suspended in its own time. This impression is confirmed by Jack's description of a shovel "in the centre of a large round stain of dried cement" in the cellar as "like the hour hand of a big broken clock" (97). In addition, he has earlier wondered how the energetic and organized Commander Hunt in the novel Sue has given him would behave if, instead of traveling through the universe at speed, his space ship "had remained perfectly still, fixed in outer space"

(91–92). Once again, the novel is aiming at a generality of reference. What the reader sees are not just one family's aberrations, or even just one nation's (although the events of the novel chart both). When the outraged Derek asks Julie and Jack how long their incestuous relationship has been going on, she answers, "Ages . . . ages and ages" (150). The suggestion of timelessness applies not just to their relationship, but to the whole action of the text.

Place, too, manages to be both quite specific and yet strangely unlocalized and general. When Jack describes the area around his house, it is at once recognizable to anyone who grew up in 1960s urban Britain, and yet at the same time, a generic postwar city waste-land (27–28). Once again, this functions to generalize the novel's action. However, although the precise location of the novel's setting may finally remain unspecified, the features of that setting are very clear. It is one of utter decay and disorder. Early in the novel, Jack describes how his father's ornamental garden falls into decay. "Weeds pushed through the cracks in the paving stones, part of the rockery collapsed and the little pond dried up. The dancing Pan fell on its side and broke in two and nothing was said" (21). Later he gives further details of the house's desolate surroundings. The "four twenty-storey tower blocks" nearby "stood on wide aprons of cracked asphalt where weeds were pushing through. They looked even older and sadder than our house. All down their concrete sides were colossal stains, almost black, caused by the rain. They never dried out" (29). Jack walks around a fire-gutted prefab and notes the devastation, the weeds growing in the rooms; "In this burned-out place there was no order," he notes (47). After the mother's death, the kitchen becomes "a place of stench and clouds of flies" (82), an image which will be repeated later in the text (135).

The ultimate motif of decay comes when the mother's corpse begins to rot in the ill-made tomb. The text presents this in some detail. First Jack notices a smell about his own person (121). Shortly afterward, Jack and Sue inspect the tin trunk in the cellar. "The trunk looked like it had been kicked. The middle bulged right out. The surface of the concrete was broken by a huge crack in some places half an inch wide. . . . I leaned over the crack at its widest point and shone the torch down. I saw a convoluted, yellowish-grey surface. Round the edge was something black and frayed. As I stared the surface formed itself briefly into a face, an eye, part of a nose and a dark mouth. The image dissolved into convoluted surfaces once more" (131–32). And things do not improve. In the course of the novel, no ordering, restoring force comes. Jack describes his bedroom on the last day of the novel's action. "On the floor were Coca-Cola tins, dirty clothes, fish and chip wrappers, several wire coat-hangers, a box that once contained rubber bands. . . . Under the bed I found plates and cups covered in green mold" (141). The world of *The Cement Garden* is one of unremitting decay.

Characters, like time and place, are at once very physically and substantially there and at the same time rather general. Names alone indicate their generic quality. The mother and father are never named; the reader never learns the family's surname. He/she does not learn Jack's name until page 32, and when it is given, it comes as a kind of joke on the part of the implied author, "to jack off" being an informal synonym for "to masturbate." Even outsiders, Derek, Mr. and Mrs. Oswald (actually reduced to initial status as Mr. and Mrs. O. [113–14]), and the others at the snooker hall are simple, fairly generic characters. Jack's confusion concerning the woman on the bridge (is it his mother, or Julie, or a stranger?) suggests the everyperson nature of characters in the text (83–84). Once again, this is a universalizing device in the novel, but it also stems from the extreme solipsism of Jack the narrator's point of view. He is scarcely one to explore the complexities of another character, since he is so reluctant to examine his own motives. Characters are vividly sketched with a few physical details, and it is left pretty much at that: the father with clipboard and pipe (ch. 1); the mother with her fatigue and set phrases (34–35, 58–59); Sue with her diary and books; Julie with her beauty, brown skin, and athleticism; Tom with his snot and whining; Derek with his flashy suit, coat, and sports car (112, 129–30). Even Jack himself is, as a result of the text's strangely detached narrational strategy, finally a shadowy figure, despite the lavish detail concerning his acne and masturbation.

Three sets of images are continually expressed through the characters: images of physical unpleasantness, of male-female tension, and of exclusion and inclusion. As a corollary to the urban decay and desolation which surrounds the children's house, the novel is replete with references to physiological processes that are traditionally taboo or viewed as unsavory. One reviewer links together the "stinks, garbage, weeds, corpses, pus and wasted sperm with which the book is strewn."[5] Jack's minute description of his ejaculate can be viewed in this way (23), as can his frequent comments on the "humps and pits of my complexion" (27). "I was trying to grow a beard to conceal my skin," he informs the reader, "yet each of the sparse hairs led the eye like a pointing finger to the spot at its base" (43). Julie urinates in the bed when Jack tickles her brutally (37); Jack recalls when "Tom did a shit in his pants and a rare, sharp smell drifted upstairs" (78). One is given the details of Tom's nasal mucus; for example, Jack observes how he "brought something from his nose on the end of his forefinger, glanced at it and wiped it on a chair cushion" (100).

In part, characters are clearly divided in terms of gender. The novel starts with what Jack sees as a wonderfully male episode when the workmen deliver the cement. Laconic, grunting, aggressive, mysteriously purposeful, the participants in this scene fill Jack with admiration. "I liked this kind of talk," he remarks apropos the men's grunts. "I did not wish to be placed outside this intense community of work," he reveals, and stands at his unloved and unlovable father's side as he signs for the cement (14). The ornamental garden, all insane neatness and symmetry, is solely the father's work (19); he wishes to concrete over the whole garden because "it will be tidier" (21). While Jack and he work on making the cement, Jack notes that "for once I felt at ease with him" (22). When Derek appears on the scene, he attempts to win Jack for a kind of masculine solidarity. He takes him to the predominantly male world of the snooker hall, and even confides in him there, "Strictly man to man, you understand?" (118). Later he offers paternally to teach Jack how to mix cement properly (134). Jack himself represents aspects of the male sphere in the text—ugly, selfish, potentially and actually violent, constantly masturbating. "Do boys do that all the time?" Sue asks him at one point (106). In the text, it certainly seems part of being male.

All this contrasts markedly with the female sphere in the text. The mother is "a quiet sort of person" (15), associated with feeding the family, with rest, concern, and gentle ineffectuality. After the father's death, she and Julie have "long conversations" in the kitchen "that would break off if Tom, Sue or I came in suddenly" (36). Julie herself is, on one level, the antithesis of Jack, beautiful where he is ugly, athletic where he is torpid. Indeed, the entire text could be viewed as charting a passage from rigid male control, the cement garden, to a much freer, if anarchic, state, whose presiding deities are the mother and Julie.

Of course, the division between male and female in the novel is not rigid. Jack deeply dislikes his authoritarian father. He deliberately makes him help to carry heavy weights although he knows this to be dangerous to the older man's health (18). He conspires with Julie to mock the father's garden (20). Despite the community of work between father and son, Jack soon gets bored, thinks of his sisters, and goes off to masturbate (22–23). Tom particularly feels the disadvantages of such a division. He works out the advantages of being a girl rather than a boy ("Because you don't get hit when you're a girl" [54]) and goes further by persuading his sisters to dress him as a girl (86–87). Thereafter he slips in and out of two gender roles, happily wearing girls' clothes at times and playing with one of his friends in them (96). The scene in which Sue and Julie first dress Tom up as a girl reveals Jack's own unease in the highly polarized male-female world. "How easy it was to become someone else," he thinks. "I crossed my arms and hugged myself. . . . I was excited and scared" (86). Julie clearly notices this. "Here's another one," she says, "who's tired of being a grumpy boy" (86). In the last analysis, perhaps Jack and Julie's sexual intercourse at the novel's end *is* a kind of maturing initiation for Jack. He and Julie, male and female, literally and metaphorically come together in a process stressing equality and balance, the uniting of seeming opposites (151).

Although the male-female polarization of the world of *The Cement Garden* is not rigid, it does seem the source and expression

of most of the tensions that run through the characters and their relationships. Certainly, there are tensions among the male characters.
The invalid father competes with Tom for the mother's attention
(17). Jack's hostility toward his father is clear from the opening
words of the novel, and his antagonism toward Derek eventually
takes its place. Indeed, Jack's Oedipal rejection of father figures is
so obviously present as almost to be a comic, parodic element in the
text. (A Freudian reading of the novel's characters is advanced by
the French critics Gérard Klaus and Max Duperray.[6] However,
Jack's is no formulaic Oedipal complex; his lust is for his sister, not
for his mother.) But right from the start, the reader is aware of a
grinding hostility between male and female. When the cement produces a quarrel between father and mother, the father responds to the
mother's reasonable objections (they do not have enough money for
this project) with a laconic and offensive brutality. "While my
mother talked my father used a penknife to scrape black shards from
the bowl of his pipe on to the food he had barely touched" (15).

Jack's treatment of his mother—ignoring her and using her,
refusing her affection—is part of the novel's general polarization of
male and female (27, 31–32). Jack, to some extent, plays his father's
role after his death. The reader observes his male aggression toward
Julie and his adoption of his father's role when he frightens and violently tickles his sister. To do so he slips on "a pair of huge, filthy
gardening gloves, last worn by my father" (36). Sue's diary reveals
just how violent a figure Jack has become (109). Derek himself
wants to dominate the children, to assume the role of a father with
them. "He wants to be one of the family, you know, big smart
daddy. He's getting on my nerves," Julie tells Jack (148). Julie also

FICTION AND EVIL (I)

reveals the irony that Derek comes from a background in which he is utterly subject to his mother.

The third chain of images expressed through characters involves exclusion and inclusion. The pattern is observable both within the family and in its relations with the outside world. Exclusion and isolation predominate. The novel starts with what is for Jack an ambiguous moment of both exclusion and inclusion. Initially rejected from the adult male world of work (he is reading a comic rather than the sports page of a newspaper; he cannot answer the workmen quickly enough), he is finally included in "this intense community of work" which exists between his father and the workmen (13–14). But motifs of exclusion rapidly come to dominate the text. Before his heart attack, the father had intended "to build a high wall round his special world" that is the house and garden (19). By his attitude toward his daughter's running, the father excludes himself from the family group who watches Julie's success. "He missed the pale-brown, slim legs flickering across the green like blades, or me, Tom, Mother and Sue running across the enclosure to cover Julie with kisses when she took her third race" (25). Julie herself, following "an unspoken family rule," never brings friends home (26). When Jack and his mother plan his birthday party, they decide just to have family there. Jack recalls that his father's bossiness and obsession with order led to any parties, and thus any visitors' coming to the house, being put a stop to (41).

Exclusion is marked not just in the family's relations with the outside world, but within it as well. After Jack behaves boorishly to his mother, the others shun him (28–30). He feels himself excluded from Julie's and his mother's conversations (36). When Julie lumps him in with the others as "you lot," he resents it immediately (60). As his sisters cry at their mother's death, he feels "excluded" (62), and he feels a similar emotion when watching them dress Tom as a girl (86). The only time Jack feels included in the family group is at his birthday party when Julie's marvelous handstand leads him to sing the song they had asked him to (45), and when he and his sisters clean up the disorderly house. "For the first time in weeks I was happy. I felt safe, as if I belonged to a powerful, secret army" (95). But as the novel progresses, Jack is again and again excluded or excludes himself from the family group, by his jealousy of Derek (107) or by his own violence (122). When Derek arrives on the scene, he too feels excluded. He tries to penetrate the family secret and is rebuffed. His taking Jack to the snooker hall (111–20) and his working in the cellar (138) are all unavailing attempts to have the family trust him and include him. "I wish you would all . . . well, trust me a little more" (140). His ultimate moment of exclusion comes when he finds Jack and Julie naked in bed together (150). But Derek's exclusion marks Jack's reinclusion into the family. Lying next to the sleeping Tom, he and Julie are reunited. After Derek starts smashing the trunk in the cellar, Sue joins them, and they all wait together for the forces of law and order which will, ironically, break up the family (152).

As with the family tensions discussed above, exclusion seems to be male-driven in *The Cement Garden*. The father's manic orderliness and desire for authority, Jack's boorishness and violence, and Derek's desire to play the "big smart daddy" (148) all lead to their exclusion from others, from the female family members. Only as a naked child, and in terms of gentleness and equality (or even submission, for Julie initiates their intercourse), can Jack find inclusion.

FICTION AND EVIL (I)

In this respect, too, *The Cement Garden* shows itself to be clearly critical of traditional male behavior.

Above all, *The Cement Garden* depicts a collapse of norms, rules, and order. To some extent, these rules are included in the text; however, in some measure the novel relies on the implied reader's cultural knowledge to provide the norms against which the characters' actions may be viewed. When his father proposes covering the garden in cement, Jack is excited by the idea and sees it as a "fascinating violation" (21). This might stand as a rubric for the rest of the novel, which provides a series of such fascinating violations. Once the mother becomes bed-ridden, the children "adapted well enough" to new patterns of behavior different from the old norms (49). For Jack the mother's possible departure to the hospital brings "a sense of freedom" (58), and her actual death brings real freedom, coinciding as it does with the beginning of the school holidays (59). After her burial (itself a breach of social norms) Jack recalls one of the few occasions when the children had been left alone previously, and the daylong, far from unpleasant anarchy that was brought with it (for all except Tom) (79–80). Tom's dressing as a girl is also a breach of social rules, although none of his friends seems to react to it as such, a response which, however, in turn surprises Jack (93–96). The house is allowed to degenerate into a disorder of decayed food and dirt, while the children spend their days to no traditionally approved of purpose: in play, in escapist reading, in sleep, in masturbation. Jack's dream, in which he cannot stop masturbating in front of a physically reduced mother, well expresses this kind of social violation (105–6). Such breaches continue throughout the text. Tom does not just become a girl but also reverts to babyhood. Violation follows upon violation. At the conclusion, three of the children are naked, Jack has joined Tom in partial babyhood, and Jack and Julie have committed incest. Julie reveals that she despises Derek at least in part because he does follow rules (147–48).

It is noticeable that Jack and his brothers and sisters scarcely feel that their actions are reprehensible. The world of *The Cement Garden* is one in which traditional norms seem not to apply. "What was wrong with me?" Jack wonders (83), but his question is weak and possibly ironic. Later, as he inspects his mother's tomb, it is his uncertainty about the immorality or abnormality of his actions that is striking (98). When in a dream his mother upbraids him in his father's name for masturbating, Jack responds by saying, "But you're both dead" (106). Their standards simply have no validity. The children certainly do clean up the kitchen on one occasion (94–96), and Jack even tidies his room after a fashion (141). But these partial restorations of order are not motivated by any sense of rules or norms, but rather by a desire for unity in the first case and simply for change in the latter. The nakedness, infantile regression, and incest that conclude the novel are not seen as deviant acts by the participants themselves. The absence of rules and norms is not felt as a burden by them, but rather at times as a liberation, or as something in itself perfectly normal and natural. "The impossibility of knowing or feeling anything for certain gave me a great urge to masturbate," Jack declares (98). It does not throw him into moral despair. As he and his sister lie naked together, he feels no shame, no breach of rules. Indeed, the whole experience is unalloyed and positive. "I felt weightless, tumbling through space with no sense of up or down" (149).

The Cement Garden presents a striking picture of how people can behave not immorally, but in ways that are indifferent to normally accepted standards. In doing so, it offers what one can view as an even more frightening image of human potential. The children are not evil or immoral; they simply seem indifferent to the rules and norms of their wider society and of most readers' culture. Such people, the reader is left to conclude, would be capable of anything under the right circumstances.

And those people are here, now, in England. The pressure toward a British national-political reading of *The Cement Garden* is less strong than in, for example, Graham Swift's *Shuttlecock* (1981) or Kazuo Ishiguro's *The Remains of the Day* (1989), but it is still present. The typical urban wasteland of 1960s Britain in which the novel is set and the crabbed and authoritarian father whose death along with that of the children's other parent sets the protagonists free (if only temporarily) carry a political and social resonance. The Commander Hunt, whom Jack reads about and whose nobility and purpose he rejects, sounds very like the kind of stalwart British-English hero from the early– and mid–twentieth century (Biggles? Dan Dare?) who was meant to inspire a feckless postwar British youth (91). It seems possible to read *The Cement Garden* not just as a highly generalized account of childhood indifference to social norms, but as a depiction of a specifically British rejection of a sterile authoritarian and patriarchal past. In this respect, it is worth noting that the restoration of order at the end by the police eerily prefigures the attempted recovery and reimposition of traditional values that marked British political life in the 1980s. *The Cement Garden* aims for, and achieves, a timelessness, but it is also a text very much for its own time, a kind of mini twisted "Condition-of-England" novel.[7]

CHAPTER FOUR

Fiction and Evil (II)
The Comfort of Strangers

As in *The Cement Garden*, McEwan combines in *The Comfort of Strangers* (1981) a fictional technique that continually draws attention to itself with a concern with human evil, thus maintaining the dual focus of the earlier novel. Once again, one is struck by the superficial slimness of the material with which the author achieves so much.

The Comfort of Strangers, again like its predecessor, tells a rather sordid tale. An unmarried English couple, Colin and Mary, holidaying in an unnamed foreign city that bears a strong resemblance to Venice, falls in with an older couple, Robert and Caroline. The latter begin to dominate the lives of the protagonists, eventually murdering Colin and (presumably) having some kind of sex over his dead body in front of the drugged but conscious Mary. Mary survives to speculate on the motives underlying this fatal encounter.

Despite its provocative and salacious subject matter, the novel's reception was positive. Anthony Thwaite praises it and describes it, as other critics do, as an advance on *The Cement Garden*. J. R. Banks sees it as moving beyond what he takes to be the immature obsessions of McEwan's earlier work; he calls it "a serious, haunting and exciting story." Christopher Ricks devotes a long article to the novel, placing it in the August context of Ruskin, James, and Shakespearean tragedy, and Richard P. Brinker in *The New York Times Book Review* also takes McEwan's text seriously, relating it to James again and to Pinter. "It is a fine novel," declares James Campbell in the world quite separately. Indeed, the novel emphasizes this. As they wander the empty streets of the city, Mary inspects mannequins and a bed in a department-store window; Colin passes on to look at a book of carpet samples (21–22). Sitting in the square waiting for a coffee, they have quite divergent perspectives on the same world (49). The two other principal characters, Robert and Caroline, are presented, by and large, only as they appear to Colin and Mary through direct speech and physical description. Each is allowed fairly extensive narrative, however (31–40, 109–13), and in Robert's case, this assumes a degree of separateness and independence.

Nevertheless, the entire novel is not given from its characters' points of view. Rather, the reader is aware of a third-person narrator quite distinct from any of the characters. This figure, too, appears from the novel's start, able to provide insight into and comments on character and situation which are not those of any of the figures involved. The passage from chapter 1 beginning, "Alone, perhaps, they could each have explored the city with pleasure" (13) might be an example of Colin and Mary's shared thoughts, but it seems more reasonable to class it as the observation of a detached narrator-figure. Similarly, the passage in chapter 2 on maps of the city does not seem to belong to either Colin or Mary, but rather to a narrator who is superior to both (19–20). Indeed, a substantial number of descriptions and observations can be attributed to this figure. For example, the description of Caroline ("Her mouth, for example, was no more than the word suggested, a moving, lipped slit beneath her nose") in chapter 6 (66) is surely that of a narrator, not of Mary. In chapter 7, the narrator makes his presence felt in his succinct and prefiguring comment on Colin's and Mary's concerns about their relationship: "It was not an unreasonable fear" (82). Even where the reader encounters Colin's and Mary's feelings, the formality of style frequently suggests a detached observer and commentator. "They remained sitting for half an hour, by their slight frowns in private versions of an argument that would have been difficult to define. They were inhibited by a feeling that these past few days had been nothing more than a form of parasitism, an unacknowledged conspiracy of silence disguised by so much talk" (92).

For large parts of the novel, however, one is aware of the narrator largely through the absence of any identification with any character's point of view. The narration is frequently objective, limited to observable, external details. Even moments of great importance and emotional intensity are narrated from the outside (84–85, 90).

Ultimately, the text's narration achieves quite a complex effect. It certainly gives the protagonists' points of view, but also continually withdraws from any kind of full identification with them. It is at once knowing and detached. (This duality is further reinforced by the text's persistent narrational strategy of recounting speech indirectly. Crucial conversations, such as those in the bar between Robert and Colin and Mary (28–29) or between Colin and Mary themselves (79–81) are done in this manner, heightening one's sense of the narrator's detachment and the reader's own partial detachment from character and situation.) The text's narration creates a sense of coolness toward events and characters, a detachment that allows their predicament to be seen in particular and general terms. It also suggests the principal characters' own knowledge of each other and themselves, bred over seven years of intimacy, and yet their more than equal lack of knowledge of self and partner, their sleepwalking, collusive entry into Robert and Caroline's intrigue and fantasy. (Compare Ricks's discussion of the protagonists' "unknowing intimacy.")[3] However, as in *The Cement Garden*, such a narrational strategy may also have a self-referential function, continually reminding the reader of the narrator's presence (and in this novel, narrator and implied author are identical). To narrate dialogue indirectly, to recount moments of passion and intensity in a detached and formal manner, is to draw attention to the narrator's presence in the text, to suggest that, among other things, the text is a virtuoso display of narrational technique. The reader is constantly reminded of the artistry of the account and never allowed to immerse him/herself entirely in character and action.

Also, as in *The Cement Garden*, stylistic aspects of *The Comfort of Strangers* reinforce the text's self-referential focus. In this novel style is, as always, a multifunctional element, but one of its most prominent functions is to emphasize artistry and to draw attention to the novel's fictional status. The concluding scene of the text, in which Mary inspects Colin's dead body in a morgue, is typical (126–27). Stylistically the passage is quite mixed. It moves from some relatively neutral sections (the opening sentence, for example, or "After an hour he entered with a nurse") to others of considerable lexical and syntactic sophistication ("her theory, tentative at this stage, of course . . ." or "brought alive its referent"). Such stylistic sophistication and formality recurs throughout the text, for example, in the passage about the city's maps that begins chapter 2 (19). Here the phrase "confluences of major streets" certainly gives a formal coloring to the passage, but so, too, does the sentence's length and complexity (multiple subordinate clauses), while even such vocabulary as "draped" or "tiers" gives the passage a slight stylistic shift upward. Examples of this stylistic tendency might be multiplied. Indeed, in chapter 4 the narrator is compelled to signal—"it had once been written" (48)—that he is quoting a description of the city's cathedral (from Ruskin, although he does not say so), for otherwise the full ironic force of the juxtaposition of baby with drool and diaper and the cathedral's architecture might be lost. Stylistically, the passage from Ruskin is not entirely dissimilar to many of the narrator's own descriptions.

This stylistic complexity serves several purposes. It adds to a sense of detachment from the particular experience in the novel and to a sense of its general nature. The text not only charts a story of two couples' destructive fantasies, but also asks its readers to see it in the context of male-female relationships generally, in a detached manner to which such a sophisticated style might be appropriate. Toward the novel's end, the narrator indirectly comments on (as well as clearly embodies) his own recurrent stylistic tendency when he describes Mary's statements to the police and the impression they create. "Her lack of affect augmented the suspicion. In the assistant commissioner's office she was complimented on the precision and logical consistency of her statement, on its avoidance of distorting emotion" (124). However, the stylistic means employed by the narrator are also a self-advertising device, focusing attention on the act of narration itself, and thus have a self-referential function. To narrate moments of crisis such as a woman's examining her dead lover's body or her providing an account to the police of the events which led to his death, within a stylistic configuration which contains a sentence like "Her lack of affect augmented suspicion," is to divert attention from what is being narrated to the means employed and constantly to remind the reader of the act of narration itself.

The presentation of time and place in *The Comfort of Strangers* augments the generalizing effect of style and narrational technique.

Time and especially space are at once quite particular and yet also strangely unplaced and general. In this respect, the novel resembles *The Cement Garden* with its vivid yet unspecified modern urban wasteland setting. In *The Comfort of Strangers* the time is an unspecified present. Mary's, Colin's, and Robert's clothes, Mary's yoga, and Colin and Mary's mores (their semidetached relationship, their marijuana smoking) all point to a time very near the novel's date of publication, even though no year is given in the text. More local time-markers indicating day and hour are given throughout, but scarcely emphasized. The reader knows that Colin and Mary have been a couple for some seven years, but this is virtually the novel's only temporal signpost (77).

The characters do, however, have an important and complex relationship with time. Colin and Mary are remarkably vague about it. Mary feels that she is sleepwalking through her life (18), and both she and Colin can be extremely indefinite about past events. They seem reluctant to discuss their pasts, and, when they do, the narrator presents their accounts so indirectly as to leach these memories of almost all force (29, 74–75, 79). The narrator reduces Colin's narrative of his past to two sentences (the longer in indirect speech). Colin and Mary cannot agree on whether or when they visited a certain attraction in the city (24–25), and even when confronted with someone else's very tangible past—the cemetery island which recurs throughout the text—they see it not as a place of the dead, but as a futuristic cityscape (43). Their holiday—removing themselves from nation, language, family, home—and, indeed, their conduct while on holiday (they spend large amounts of time shut up in their hotel room)seem to imply an attempt to escape time and the past too. The city's history, clearly one of its primary sources of attraction, is completely de-emphasized in the novel. Colin and Mary inhabit their bedroom, swim in the sea, and walk a few late-night streets, but scarcely engage with the richness of the past that surrounds them. While looking at an old building, Mary sees only a prison (49).

Time and the past, however, burden Robert and Caroline. As opposed to Colin and Mary, both give (in direct speech) extended accounts of events in their past which have determined their present. Robert insists to Mary that his meeting his wife can be explained only in terms of his family background (29), while Caroline with her injured back bears the marks of the past vividly with her at all times. Robert himself is clearly haunted by the past. Indeed, his apartment is a monument to it, a kind of "family museum" full of portraits and artifacts weighed down by the past (58–59), and he must show each item to Colin and explain its provenance and history (69–71). To Colin he also bemoans the passing of a time of male dominance and certainty (71–72). The cemetery island, where Robert's father and grandfather are buried, is clearly visible from the apartment (60). One might argue that through Robert and Caroline, the past catches up with Colin and Mary.

If time is presented in a complex way in *The Comfort of Strangers*, the same is even truer with regard to place. The city in the novel is clearly Venice, but it is never named. It is vividly present and actual but is also a generalized location. The sights, sounds, and smells of the city are presented in concrete fashion throughout—the customers at cafés, the sounds of cleaning barges, the kiosks, the shop-window displays, the orchestras on the great square, the sea-side and its visitors. The reader is constantly reminded of a life going on beyond the windows of Colin and Mary's hotel room and outside Robert and Caroline's apartment. Even as the novel reaches its violent climax, Mary can hear the sounds of other lives going on around her (120). Horror and evil are placed squarely in the heart of the everyday.

The city is also marked by one other prominent feature: incomprehensibility. Colin bemoans that he and Mary keep getting lost (63), and everything in the city conspires to confuse, obscure, and mislead. At least, it has this effect on the novel's protagonists. Colin and Mary cannot understand where the barges outside their hotel go or why they are cleaned every afternoon (9). The maid who tidies their room is an almost unseen, shadowy figure, her operations an obscure magic (11–12). The maps of the city seem superficially designed to lead the tourist astray, while the people in the dark kiosks who sell them could be either male or female (19). Of course, the language is unknown to Colin and Mary (30), but, also, children's chanting could either be "a religious formula or an arithmetical table" (42), and a shake of the head could mean yes or no (51). The life in the other hotel rooms, the aria from *The Magic Flute*, and the sounds of everyday living are products of a hidden, unknown life (85). Robert himself embodies this hidden, obscure element in the text. What are his designs on Colin? What is the importance of the photograph he lets Mary see? Is the sound Colin and Mary hear when they leave the apartment a slap or merely a dropped object (76)? The quality of the incomprehensible attaches itself to Colin and Mary, too. They are not sure themselves why they are at odds with each other (9); Colin stays in Robert's apartment despite having been struck by him (72–73); at the novel's conclusion, Colin cannot understand Mary's warning (118).

In a way that is both hidden and obvious, the city is Venice and yet not Venice. On one hand, it is clearly Venice, a Venice at least partly familiar from travel writing, films, and fiction. The labyrinthine streets, the sea, and the tourists all indicate the novel's setting (although one should note that there are no gondolas, canals, churches, or art in Colin and Mary's Venice, perhaps to help emphasize their attempts to sequester themselves from life and time). One is, however, left in no doubt about where the novel's action takes place when Colin and Mary visit the city's great square (46). It is very clearly the Piazza San Marco, and the paraphrase of Ruskin that follows two pages later makes the identification conclusive (48). The narrator's major omission from the original is to suppress Ruskin's reference to the Lido.[4]

The text goes out of its way to fix the setting as Venice, yet teasingly withdraws from any specific reference. Why? This combination of specificity and vagueness, of a teasing nine-tenths acknowledgment of setting with its denial, functions in three ways in the text. First, it embodies the intrigue, the deception, the trap at the novel's heart. Just as one cannot trust appearances, just as the comfort-bringing strangers turn out to be murderers, so one can never be entirely certain of the city of the novel's setting (which, in any case, is a particularly dubious place). At the last moment it withdraws from certain identification. Second, as is usually the case when setting is unspecified, the failure to name the city functions to generalize the novel's action. This is not just a sinister sequence of actions that belongs to Venice, but perhaps to any strange place, to any unknowable setting. Finally, the nature of the novel's setting may have a self-referential function, as well as involving *The Comfort of Strangers* in a complex intertextual web. For by naming and not naming the city, the text can draw on all the literary resonances of Venice without wholly subscribing to what is, by the late twentieth century, something of a literary cliché. This aspect of Venice as literary topos had already been noticed by Henry James in his essay "Venice" (1882),[5] and has certainly become very marked a hundred years later. By not quite naming the city, McEwan both draws attention to the cliché and refreshes a setting that might otherwise be automatized and dead.

As is the case with *The Cement Garden*, *The Comfort of Strangers* is a deeply allusive work, allusive to a whole range of twentieth-century and earlier texts that have chosen Venice as a setting. A number of critics have commented on this aspect of the text, for example, Banks, Max Duperray, and Ricks, but the subject has not hitherto been fully explored.[6]

However teasingly imprecise the novel's setting is, it does involve a complex intertextuality. The Ruskin semiquotation, mentioned above, is one element in this allusiveness to earlier texts, and Ricks sees further references to Ruskin in the novel's presentation of the terrible and the grotesque (14). For the Venice which Colin and Mary visit is only tangentially part of the healthy, natural, restorative Italy of E. M. Forster's *A Room with a View* (1908). If there is any reference to Forster, it is to the sinister and, for English visitors, highly disruptive Italy of "The Story of a Panic." As critics have noted, McEwan's city is the macabre Venice of Henry James's *The Aspern Papers* (1888), Daphne du Maurier's "Don't Look Now"(1971), and Thomas Mann's *Der Tod in Venedig* (1912). In *The Aspern Papers* the death's-head-like appearance of Miss Bordereau and the two women protagonists' secluded life are echoed in Colin's macabre murder and in his and Mary's attempts to cut themselves off from life. "Don't Look Now" contains motifs of ambiguity (the weird sisters' possible transvestism, the murderer's disguise), of getting lost, of bizarre death and murder (the knife, the blood at the story's conclusion) that all recur in *The Comfort of Strangers*. In addition, du Maurier's protagonists, John and Laura, have the same kind of everyperson names and natures as Colin and Mary, while there is more than a hint in the earlier text of the male protagonist's willing his own destruction, as, at least to an extent, Colin and Mary do.

It is, however, to Thomas Mann's famous novella that McEwan's novel seems most allusive. The combination of death with homo-erotic elements is common to both texts. Tadzio and Colin are extremely beautiful and are pursued by older men. In both cases the pursuit ends in death, although of von Aschenbach (the pursuer) in Mann's novella and of Colin (the pursued) in McEwan's novel. The song which Colin and Mary and later Colin alone hear in Robert's bar is a clear allusion to *Der Tod in Venedig*. "The song they were all listening to, for no one was talking, was loud and chirpily senti-mental, with full orchestral accompaniment, and the man who sang it had a special sob in his voice for the frequent chorus which fea-tured a sardonic "ha ha ha," and it was here that several of the young men lifted their cigarettes and, avoiding each other's eyes, joined in with a frown and a sob of their own." (28)

Sitting on the hotel veranda, von Aschenbach, the protagonist of Mann's novella, is entertained, along with the other guests, by a group of musicians. Their final song strikingly resembles the juke-box hit played in Robert's bar.

> Es war ein Lied, das jemals gehört zu haben der Ein-same sich nicht erinnerte; ein dreister Schlager in unverständlichem Dialekt und ausgestattet mit einem

Lachrefrain, in den die Bande regelmässig aus vollem
Halse einfiel. Es hörten hierbei sowohl die Worte wie
auch die Begleitung der Instrumente auf, und nichts
blieb übrig, als ein rhythmisch irgendwie geordnetes,
aber sehr natürlich behandeltes Lachen, das
namentlich der Soloist mit grossem Talent zu
täuschendster Lebendigkeit zu gestalten wusste.[7] (It
was a song which the lonely von Aschenbach could
not recall ever having heard before; a bold popular
song in an incomprehensible dialect and provided
with a laughing refrain which the troupe regularly
gave out at the tops of their voices. At that point both
the words and the instrumental accompaniment
ceased, and nothing remained but a somehow rhyth-
mically ordered, but very naturally presented laugh-
ter, which the soloist in particular was able, with great
talent, to give the most deceptive liveliness to.)[8]

Further echoes of *Der Tod in Venedig* lie in Colin and Mary's complicity in their own destruction, in their sleepwalking-like acquiescence in Robert's plans. Von Aschenbach, even more clearly than
Colin and Mary, is aware of the self-destructive path he is following. "Er will es und will es nicht" (He wishes it and does not wish
it), the narrator says of Aschenbach's staying in Venice (37). "Den-
noch kann man nicht sagen, dass er litt. Haupt und Herz waren ihm
trunken, und seine Schritte folgten den Weisungen des Dämons,
dem es Lust ist, des Menschen Vernunft und Würde unter seine
Füsse zu treten" (51) (But one cannot say that he was suffering. His
head and heart were intoxicated, and his steps were following the

directions of the daemon whose pleasure it is to trample human reason and dignity underfoot). At one point the narrator calls Venice
"halb Fremdenfälle" (51) (half a trap for strangers), and the orgy of
violent sex which follows Colin's murder in *The Comfort of
Strangers* (122–23) perhaps imitates von Aschenbach's fevered sexual fantasies toward the German novella's end (61–62). (Ian McEwan
acknowledges an interest in Mann's fiction in an interview in
1978.)[9]

In addition, the Venetian setting and Colin and Mary's artsy
London background make it tempting to see some echoes of Harold
Pinter's contemporary play *Betrayal* (1978) in *The Comfort of
Strangers*. Gothic elements, too, are present in McEwan's novel.
Robert's sudden appearance "as if summoned" (25), his dress and
body (black shirt, razor-blade pendant, his body hair, his "cloying"
aftershave), the intrigue in which he involves Colin and Mary, the
cemetery island in the background, and Colin's macabre death—all
point to the novel's gothic provenance, alongside its connection
with psychological and crime fiction.

The functions of such intertextuality and generic echoes are
varied and complex. The novel's gothic elements are used to emphasize the intrusion of past into present and the eruption of the brutal
and the macabre into the seemingly everyday. Duperray argues that
McEwan's gothic, recounted without excitement, surrounded by
trivial contemporary mores and ambitions, a kind of package-tour
excursion into the unfamiliar, marks a deliberate (and metaliterary)
"banalisation" (rendering banal) of the genre and a comment on the
exhaustion of its conventions.[10] Certainly, in the late twentieth century, the full-fledged gothic genre seems thoroughly automatized
and scarcely acceptable as such within any literary hierarchy, but

McEwan's deployment of it as part of a generic mosaic seems quite typical of his generation of writers (compare Graham Swift in *Waterland* [1983] as well as Peter Ackroyd in *Hawksmoor* [1985], for example). That McEwan handles it with caution, surrounding it with the banal and the trivial, presenting it very obliquely and with great detachment of tone, does not remove its effectiveness nor the shocking violence of its final eruption into the novel. Such a treatment also functions as a metaliterary comment on the gothic and as an attempt to refresh an at least partly automatized and stale genre.

The allusion to Ruskin in *The Comfort of Strangers* (mentioned above) has primarily an ironic function. Bringing together a small drooling child and Ruskin's rapturous description of St. Mark's creates a fine humorous juxtaposition. However, over the whole text, the pseudoquotation and its ironic context can be seen as part of a general strategy of presenting Venice, utilizing its well-worn macabre suggestiveness while not falling into cliché. If one reads further in the source of the Ruskin passage, one notices a certain appropriateness to McEwan's vision of Venice. "And what effect has this splendor on those who pass beneath it?" asks Ruskin, and then, like McEwan, he points to the Robert-and-Caroline-like corruption of Venice's population against the background of St. Mark's splendor.[11]

The echoes of Pinter's *Betrayal* may do no more than confirm the suggestions of a willed infidelity to each other in Colin and Mary's actions, but the references to Mann's *Der Tod in Venedig* are surely very important (as well as striking). They serve, as is often the case with intertextuality, to broaden and generalize the action of the novel (not just one text, but two, or several, give a similar sequence of events). They also produce a hideous irony in the text. In Mann's

FICTION AND EVIL (II)

novella, Tadzio's beauty kills von Aschenbach, or rather he dies willingly in its light; in McEwan's novel, Robert brutally murders the beautiful Colin, who has at least in part acquiesced in his own death. *The Comfort of Strangers*, even more than *The Cement Garden*, is a deliberate rewriting of a classic text, commenting on it and reworking its concerns.

The allusiveness to Mann's novella adds another layer to the cosmopolitan flavor of McEwan's text, already sophisticatedly non-insular in its quasi-Venetian setting. Such cosmopolitanism is typical of a substantial part of McEwan's output; he achieves a similar range of reference in *The Innocent* and *Black Dogs*. It is also representative of the cosmopolitanism aimed at in so many texts by McEwan's contemporaries, of which Kazuo Ishiguro's and Timothy Mo's novels provide very clear examples. This cosmopolitanism, indeed, seems a key feature of much fiction by young writers in the 1980s, an attempt to break with and counteract the widely perceived provincialism of the mid-twentieth-century British novel.[12]

The action of *The Comfort of Strangers* is certainly suitable material for a gothic text. Obsession, hatred, violence, sadism, madness, obscure perversion—all these seem luridly abnormal, at least by many traditional standards. Caroline acknowledges these standards when she talks about her increasingly violent relationship with Robert (110–11). But it is the ordinariness, the normality of what happens, that the novel emphasizes. Its action plays itself out against the background of the everyday life of the city: the sounds of people at work and in cafés, neighbors singing or preparing meals, the worn heel of a young official's shoe (120, 125, 127). Even Robert and Caroline's crime, the police inform Mary, is "wearily common" (124). As was noted above, the novel generalizes its action through setting and intertextual allusion but is also constantly doing so by other means. It wishes to make clear that despite (or even because of) its lurid outcome and trappings, it is dealing with the configuration of certain basic relationships.

The protagonists' names reveal this generalized aspect very clearly. Colin, Mary, Robert, and Caroline are fairly generic names, and all the characters are without the particularity of surnames. In addition, couples of different ages mirror each other throughout the novel. Robert and Caroline form an older reflection of Colin and Mary, but there are also the elderly couple whom Colin observes from his balcony (14–15) and the young men and women on the beach (89–95). The relationship of women to men, and vice versa, lies at the novel's center. Mary's failed marriage, the mannequins in the furniture-store window in a grotesque parody of traditional male-female roles (21–22), and the feminist posters Mary, Colin, and Robert consider (22–24) are also relevant here.

As couples reflect each other, so do fathers, sons, and daughters. These relationships, too, fall within the novel's scope. The Adrienne Rich epigraph that prefaces the novel clearly points to this; like *The Cement Garden*, *The Comfort of Strangers* is meant to be seen as a representative family drama. Colin and Mary are childlike; Robert and Caroline become parent figures to them. From the start of the novel the younger couple's life in their hotel room is a kind of irresponsible physical feast composed of sleeping, making love, and bathing, one free from the normal duties of adulthood. All the labor is done by the invisible maid, and Colin and Mary "titter like school-children" in the hotel dining room (78). Robert and Caroline become something of surrogate parents to them, directing them, feeding them, waiting for them. Caroline watches them sleep; Robert disciplines Colin. The latter himself starts to become childlike in his relationship with Mary (90). This motif of parent-child relationships can be seen in Robert too. He lives in the shadow of his father and grandfather, clearly powerful and tyrannical men. His relationships with his beautiful, gentle mother and his wife, Caroline, seem complicated mixtures of dependency and loathing. The reference to *Hamlet*, with its complex and overheated family relationships, is appropriate to this aspect of the novel (68). Colin and Mary's discussion about whether social class or patriarchy is the most powerful force in human relationships emphasizes the general nature of the events in the novel (79–80). They seem designed to illustrate Mary's quite abstract theory that it is indeed patriarchy which shapes our destinies, a point she comes back to in her reflection on the causes of Colin's death, embodying, as it does, male dreams of violence and women's of acquiescence in that violence (126).

But once the intended generality of the novel's action is established, it should be noted that it does not illustrate any particular psychological or social theory very well, except in the most diffuse fashion. The action is certainly not Freudian in any heavy-handed way, nor Oedipal except that there is hostility and ambiguity in the relationship of an older to a younger man. In no sense is Mary Robert's object of desire, nor Caroline Colin's. The action is shaped by Robert's power and violence, but Colin's being hurt (rather than Mary's) gives the lie to her theory about the events. It is notable that she remains silent when confronted with Colin's corpse and does not proffer her "explanation." In the end, one is left with a set of events intended to have a general application and to touch on some basic human relationships, but which form their own heady mixture of power, ambiguity and mutability, and complicity.

The relationships of the novel are marked by violence and by violence as an expression of power and a pursuit of power. Robert's relations with Caroline clearly illustrate this, as do those he has with his father and sisters. Colin and Mary, too, are capable of violent fantasies at least. Mary imagines having Colin's limbs amputated, retaining him only as a sexual object for her and her friends' satisfaction (81–82). Colin, on the other hand, envisages a complex machine that will inflict sexual intercourse on Mary nonstop for the rest of her life (81–82). Later one sees how Robert controls Colin by violence and firmness; he disciplines and guides him physically. Finally, he and Caroline exercise ultimate and violent power over Colin and Mary by killing one and drugging the other.

Human relationships in *The Comfort of Strangers* are also marked by a deep ambiguity, by a shifting of identity and relations. Motifs of mutability and transformation abound. In Robert's story of his childhood he is shocked by his sisters' sudden change into glamorous women (33). This shifting of identity is reflected in Colin's constantly emphasized sexual ambiguity; on several occasions he becomes almost female. His neck is "womanly" (56), and he wears a woman's frilly dressing gown in Robert and Caroline's apartment (57). At times he claims to feel "an approximation of womanly desire" (79), while Robert's treatment of him puts him in a feminine role (103–4). Just before Caroline and Robert kill him, Caroline paints Colin's lips with blood so that they "were completely and accurately rouged" (121).

One should also note that Colin and Mary's relationship oscillates between union and disunion; it is under constant threat of mutability. From the novel's beginning, their mutual dependence is emphasized. The Mozart duet, "Mann und Weib" (Man and Wife) from *The Magic Flute*, with its celebration of marital oneness, forms an appropriate (if finally ironic) background refrain to this aspect of their life together (11, 78). Their physical closeness is felt in a perfect physical familiarity (17), while their mental and emotional unity is revealed when they find themselves looking at the same objects (51). Caroline describes them as "almost like twins" (66); indeed, in their sequestered hotel room one sees them living a physical and emotional union so close that it excludes (for a time at least) the rest of the world.

Yet their relationship is also marked from the start by an incipient disunity, a threatened divergence. On the first page of the novel the reader learns that "for reasons they could no longer define clearly, Colin and Mary were not on speaking terms" (9). Half-aware that they might enjoy the city more if each were on his or her own (13), they are like the dummies in the furniture-store window, no longer quite looking fondly at each other (21–22). After their four days of seclusion, they fear, at some level, that their perfect unity may shatter, as indeed it starts to do when Mary sets off for the café alone (82–83) or when she swims out to sea (92–95). Once they return to Robert and Caroline's apartment, they are physically and permanently separated. On their way there, they "did not hold hands" (99). Their disunity both mirrors and contrasts with Caroline and Robert's relationship. Caroline is the brutalized, confined wife, but she is also the murderer's accomplice and a willing participant in her own suffering. To Mary she defines love as a complete dedication to the other's will (62).

Caroline's complicity in her own suffering further reflects Colin's and Mary's. Like her, they are both Robert's pawns and also collaborators in their own fate. To some extent, Colin and Mary seem sleepwalkers, automata guided by forces beyond their control. Mary feels and dislikes this (18). She and Colin wander the night streets of the city without real aim or purpose and are implicitly compared to the inert mannequins in a shop window (21–22). When Robert encounters them for the second time, he takes charge, and Mary lapses into her sleepwalker role once more (53). Their domination by Robert and Caroline is emphasized in Colin's walk with Robert through the city, coming at his command (105–6), and in Caroline's drugging Mary (115–16).

But when Colin and Mary first encounter Robert, their destroyer appears "as if summoned" (25). Colin even blames Mary for Robert's appearance. From the novel's start, the two protagonists are looking for the adventure that will separate them. They dress and prepare to go out "as though somewhere among the thousands they were soon to join, there waited someone who cared deeply how they appeared" (11, 13). They choose to return to Robert and Caroline; they seem to walk, at least partly consciously, into their own trap (98–99, 105–6). "Still careful to avoid the other's eye, they walked towards an alleyway on their left which would bring them to the house. They did not hold hands" (99). And this has been the case throughout the novel. They could leave the city or the square, but do not do so (49–50). After being struck by Robert, Colin neither tells Mary (until much later) nor runs (72–73). Knowing it means the shattering of their union, Mary leaves the hotel room (82–83), and as she watches Robert and Caroline begin their slow sexual murder of Colin, she feels it has "every nuance of a private fantasy" (120). The question is: whose fantasy? Is it solely Robert's, or Robert's and Caroline's? Or is it at least hinted that Colin and Mary are partly complicit in their own fates? As the murderers encircle him and caress his face,

Colin stands still, unresisting, not fully understanding their intent (119–20). To what degree is this murder Colin's and Mary's own fantasy of escape, of thrill, gone terribly wrong? To consider it this way certainly makes the text's action more complex and interesting and may help to explain Mary's silence with Colin's corpse at the novel's end. Her "explanation" is only a partial one and conceals whole currents of guilt and complicity. As in *The Cement Garden*, McEwan seems able to encompass very considerable complexities within a seemingly limited scope.

CHAPTER FIVE

Change, Dystopia, and the Way Out
The Child in Time

The Child in Time (1987) is longer and has a much more complex story material than McEwan's earlier novels. Set a few years in the future from its time of publication in 1987, it centers on the main character's (Stephen Lewis, a best-selling author of novels for children) attempts to recover from the loss of his three-year-old daughter. The reader learns early in the novel that she has been abducted while shopping with her father in a local supermarket, and the loss of the daughter has led to the breakup of Stephen's marriage with his musician wife Julie. The novel's principal action begins some two years after the abduction. Stephen is involved in a British government subcommittee, which is preparing part of a report on childcare. A fairly authoritarian right-wing government has decided to make proper, disciplined childcare part of its official policy. In fact, the committee's activities are pointless because the Government's Report has already been written by Stephen's friend Charles Darke, a youngish, aspiring Conservative politician, to whom he owes his place on the subcommittee.

Darke is the center of events that interweave with Stephen's catatonic shambling through what remains of his life. Darke has caught the eye of the prime minister (whose sex is never specified), who entertains a strong affection for him. Darke himself meanwhile regresses into childhood, choosing to escape from the pressures of his life by attempting to become a ten-year-old boy. In this he is supported and protected by his physicist wife Thelma, an expert on theories of the nature of time. It is appropriate that she is so, for not only is her husband attempting to reverse time, but Stephen, too, steps out of his own time on one occasion. He has the metaphysical experience of seeing his own parents discussing him (and discussing whether to abort him) before he is born. As the novel moves toward its end, Charles effectively commits suicide, and Stephen and Julie are reunited. An earlier attempt at reconciliation has led to Julie's becoming pregnant (just after Stephen has his out-of-time experience), and now, the midwife being delayed, Stephen helps with the delivery of his own child (whose sex, it is important to note, is unspecified at the novel's end).

The differences to the pared-down action of *The Cement Garden* and *The Comfort of Strangers* could scarcely be clearer. Indeed, the above summary omits several strands of events, such as those concerning Stephen's parents; his childhood in various postwar British colonial, military posts; Darke's political career; and the political, social, and economic state of the novel's Britain. In addition, the novel's narrative organization is more intricate than the straightforward linear narratives of the previous novels. Large parts of the first third of the novel involve a movement between different times, as Stephen sits in his committee meetings recalling past events—the loss of his daughter, his life with his parents—and provide expository material from which the remainder of the novel can proceed in a chronological way.

There are other obvious differences between *The Child in Time* and McEwan's earlier novels. Its setting is not the unnamed urban wasteland of *The Cement Garden*, nor the teasingly half-specified, half-denied Venice of *The Comfort of Strangers*, but rather a London and the Home Counties, set slightly in the future and slightly transformed, for sure, but still specified and part of our documented landscape. Unlike characters in the earlier fiction, the personages of *The Child in Time* boast full names (no one has a surname in the preceding novels). In addition, the novel demonstrates an overt concern with public history; it is usually taken to be a critique of tendencies in 1980s British and, indeed, world politics. Above all, it lacks the images of bodily fluids, physical decay, horrid violence, and psychopathology that run throughout McEwan's first two novels. This last aspect is summed up by Brian Martin in the *Spectator*, who writes that "the macabre, sordid, sadistic world of McEwan's earlier novels has passed. His Gothic adolescence has given way to adult life and grown-up insights."[1]

This view is echoed elsewhere. *The Child in Time* is usually seen by critics and commentators to mark a watershed in McEwan's fiction. For example, Jack Slay, Jr., quotes McEwan's protagonist Stephen Lewis to describe the novel as "something of a departure." Judy Cooke in the *Listener* declares that it "proves to be a development from McEwan's previous fiction, a progression both technically and thematically," and Boyd Tonkin in the *New Statesman* concludes his review with the resounding judgment that "Ticketed *ad nauseam* as a master of the grotesque, he [McEwan] has drawn a Nativity that owes more to Fra Angelico than to Hieronymous Bosch." Even Gabriele Annan's negative review of the novel in the *New York Review of Books* notes that *The Child in Time* is different from the author's earlier work. "He used to go in for being extremely disgusting," she comments, "but even here the final delivery is fairly free from mess."[2]

CHANGE, DYSTOPIA, AND THE WAY OUT

The reception of *The Child in Time* has, however, been quite mixed. Several critics have praised it highly. For example, Michael Neve in the *Times Literary Supplement* calls it "a courageous and socially enraged novel;" Martin in the *Spectator* declares it "a serious novel which has many levels of intention, and provides many sources of pleasure" and "beyond doubt . . . McEwan's best yet." This praise is echoed in Cooke's article in the *Listener*: "At last, a novel which confronts the major issues of the Eighties and draws from them a rich, complicated narrative, its ideas embodied in character and situation, its style fluent and witty, engaging the reader's attention on every page." In his study Slay, too, marks it as McEwan's "finest achievement."[3]

But there have also been dissenting voices. In the *London Review of Books* Nicholas Spice suggests that "the meaning" of certain central scenes, such as Stephen's strange experience out of time, "is too designed, too clumsily obvious, and not very interesting." He finds that the novel "expends its uncommon creative energies on a program of undistinguished social and philosophical commentary." Annan in the *New York Review of Books* is even more scathing. *The Child in Time* is "rather a silly novel," she writes, and, noting in the quotation given above that it is not as disgusting as earlier novels, concludes that "what is hard to take this time is the corn."[4] The novel's conclusion particularly vexes some readers. The birth of the child and Stephen's helping to deliver it are seen as sentimental and, worse, as a manifestation of male envy of female reproductive powers. This is the gist of Adam Mars-Jones's intemperate but quite convincing attack on McEwan in his pamphlet *Venus Envy* (he also attacks Martin Amis in it). He points to the way in which Stephen constantly usurps female roles relating to childbirth: he helps his mother decide not to abort him; he saves a truck driver from a crash in a parody of birth; he delivers his own child and saves its life.[5] He describes this as "not a true indifference to gender, let alone a transcendence of it, but a temporary blurring of identities, under cover of which, the male, all the while loudly extolling the sanctity of her privileges, usurps the female."[6] Clearly, whatever changes McEwan has made in his fiction in comparison with his earlier work, he has not made it uncontroversial in *The Child in Time*.

In terms of narration, *The Child in Time* both differs from and recalls McEwan's earlier novels. On one level it poses none of the complexities of *The Cement Garden*, being narrated by a traditional third-person, anonymous narrator who, however, observes the action exclusively from the principal character Stephen's point of view. This technique is quite consistently employed throughout the text. The reader is given Stephen's feelings and thoughts directly, but never those of his wife Julie, of his friend Thelma, or indeed of her husband Charles. One passage among many can stand as an example of this. Stephen has climbed to the top of a beech tree to visit Charles's tree house. It is one of his first (and last) encounters with his friend's regression into a simulated childhood.[7] Here the point of view is quite representative of that of the novel as a whole. One is presented entirely with Stephen's perspective on things, his perceptions and feelings. The passage even contains a sentence of free indirect speech that is clearly Stephen's.

There are, however, occasions in the text where the narrator speaks in propria persona directly to the reader. For example, of Stephen's attempts to return to the time before the loss of his daughter, the narrator comments: "But time—not necessarily as it is, for who knows that, but as thought has constituted it—monomaniacally forbids second chances" (10). On the next page it is clearly the narrator, and not Stephen, who analyzes the habits of the customers of the local supermarket (11). Indeed, throughout the novel the narrator occasionally steps forward to address the reader directly. "Only when you are grown up, perhaps only when you have children yourself, do you fully understand that your own parents had a full and intricate existence before you were born" (51). Here the reflection is not Stephen's, but rather the narrator's own. This is the case, too, with the following: "Any drunk in a bar could have told Stephen that he was still in love with his wife, but Stephen was a little too clever for that, too in love with thought" (159). A certain further degree of narrational complexity arises when the reader is given an account of the early months of Stephen's parents' relationship (195–208). Supposedly this is being given to Stephen by Mrs. Lewis, but is in fact given by a third-person quasi-omniscient narrator (although he gives hardly any other point of view than that of Mrs. Lewis). The dominant narrational position is here disrupted, as it is through the narrator's intrusions. It is worth noting that these disruptions often occur at points of some emotional intensity for the characters: for example, when Julie and Stephen have come together again after a long separation (69, 71–72, 74–75); when Mrs. Lewis gives Stephen the key to his remarkable metaphysical experience of the past (195–208).

What is McEwan's aim here? Two possible (contradictory) explanations for this narrational strategy can be suggested. First, although narrational technique is not as complex as it is in McEwan's earlier novels, it does, as in them, constitute a reminder of the novel's textuality. The storyteller, the anonymous manipulator of character and situation, steps forward at these points as he does in

The Cement Garden and *The Comfort of Strangers*. Second, the narrator's intrusions in the text are quite appropriate to the traditional, third-person, anonymous narrator of the nineteenth-century British-novel tradition, such as the narrators of Charles Dickens or George Eliot novels. Or one can argue that the novel's narrational strategy shares both these functions and maintains them in some kind of compromise formation.

The narrator's language, too, is worth commenting on. A marked, if intermittent, formality of language draws attention to the act of narration in *The Child in Time*, for example, in the second paragraph of the novel (2). Vocabulary here is relatively sophisticated and formal: "a deep disposition," "an outline experience had stenciled on character," "vestiges," "dispassionate in its unstoppability," "sinewy" (in the context of clock and heart), "kept faith with an unceasing conditional," "proliferating instances," "frail, semi-opaque screen," "fine tissues of time and chance." Syntax, too, although to a lesser degree, is not without sophistication. Syntactical complexity is achieved through parenthetical insertions such as "jigging and weaving," "though barely consciously," "dispassionate in its unstoppability," and also through the presence of subordinate clauses, for example, in the last sentence of the paragraph.

Throughout the novel, often at moments of some crisis, the narrator produces a sentence of unusual and hence quite striking complexity. Thus, for example, the reader learns of Stephen's return home after losing his daughter. "There was a loud crashing music in his head, a great orchestral tinnitus whose dissonance faded as he stood there holding the banister and started up again the moment he continued" (18). Here "a great orchestral tinnitus whose dissonance faded" is certainly at the formal end of any spectrum of language.

Similarly, when after a long separation Julie and Stephen make love, vocabulary and syntax are again surprisingly formal (71). Here the sophistication needs no pointing out. There are, doubtless, numerous ways to describe sexual intercourse, but to do so in terms of "a warm, humming, softly consonated, roundly vowelled word" is rather self-consciously erudite. The same might be said for the rather archaic, intransitive use of "provide." All this stands out the more by virtue of contrast with the informal and elliptic sentence that concludes the account of the lovemaking.

Once again, one has to ask what the narrator and the author intend here. This intermittent formality of language is multifunctional: it dignifies character and action; it puts them in a broader intellectual context that is appropriate to Thelma's mini-lectures on the nature of time (45–47, 135–39). But among its functions is perhaps a self-referential one of drawing attention to the act of narration, of reminding any reader of the presence of story and storyteller (the last being all the more marked in *The Child in Time* because such shifts often occur in moments of substantial emotional crisis on the part of the characters).

Another way in which *The Child in Time* differs from its predecessors is that it is much more mixed in terms of genre. It is, to a considerable degree, like so much of McEwan's fiction, a psychological novel, presenting Stephen's and, to a lesser extent, Julie's coming to terms with the unspeakable experience of losing a child. The text focuses on the range of Stephen's actions and emotions which this traumatic event prompts, his initial activity, his retreat into alcohol and torpor, his gradual emergence from that state, and his final reunion with Julie. Although less information is given about her, the reader also follows Julie's different response to Kate's abduction. In addition, Stephen's memories of his childhood on British air-force bases in the Far and Middle East are given in a brief section of chapter 4 (76–83), as is the first account of a visit to his parents' home and all the emotional issues involved. These both add to one's sense that the novel is in part a psychological one. The relationship between Thelma and Charles is also, by implication, a difficult one, she the older intellectual wife of an ambitious businessman and politician who is bedeviled by impulses toward childlike regression. Indeed, in an almost too pat fashion Thelma sets out some of Charles's psychological conflicts (237–38), and, earlier in the novel, she has spoken of the mysteries of Charles's "inner life" (48).

Yet *The Child in Time* also shows features of the political novel. It is a novel of social-political criticism. The figure of the prime minister looms large in sections of the novel (Stephen actually meets her/him on two occasions), and Stephen himself is involved in work for a government committee, the activities of which are rendered useless by the fact that the Government (indeed, Charles Darke himself) has already written the committee's report. The particular elements of social-political criticism in the text make it, in fact, generically a dystopia. The novel is set in a Britain that is both familiar and yet subtly different from any current, documented Britain. Tendencies in that latter Britain in the 1980s are presented as achieved facts in the world of the novel. Thus, the first three pages detail the breakdown of public transport in London and an encounter with licensed beggars (1–3). The implied reader is intended to recognize both these phenomena as logical developments of British Government policy in the 1980s, especially that associated with the governments of Margaret Thatcher (1979–1990), but also to see that neither has yet become fact at the time of the novel's publication.

The world of the novel is a dystopic vision of what one might call Thatcherite Britain. The police are armed. Stephen admires "the oil and leather smell of their polished gun holsters" (17). Education is "a dingy, shrunken profession; schools were up for sale to private investors, the leaving age was soon to be lowered" (26). Ambulance companies are private businesses (194). (The force of these changes may be lost on U.S. readers; however, they are meant in 1987 to be shocking deviations from British empirical reality, although, as was suggested above, logical developments of current Government policies.) The southern English countryside has been turned into a vast conifer plantation so that Britain may be self-sufficient in wood (115, 119), and the Government has sponsored an inane all-day television channel "specializing in game and chat shows, commercials and phone-ins" (143). Only one newspaper does not support a Government that has clearly been in power for very many years (211). The national malaise is also an international one. Cold war tensions come to a boil during an Olympic Games, and the world is threatened with nuclear destruction (34–35). That the state of Britain in the novel is a malaise is indicated strongly through characters' responses to it. Both Stephen and his father pass negative judgment on the aspects of the country set out above. Mr. Lewis sums up a journey across London. "The filth on the streets, the dirty messages on the walls, the poverty, son, it's all changed in ten years. That's the last time I visited Pauline, ten years ago. It's a new country. More like the Far East at its worst. I haven't got the strength for it, or the stomach" (209). Stephen is tempted to give vent to his feelings at the end of his last encounter with the prime minister (an interview which makes the identification of the fictional prime minister, despite his/her unstated gender, and the real Mrs. Thatcher quite clear; "And you are the upholder of family values," Stephen says to him/her [222]).

Tutorial-like speculations on time and also metaphysical, supernatural experience add to the novel's genre complexity. The former are centered on Thelma and are transmitted through Stephen's perceptions and understanding. They occur on two occasions, once early in the text and once later (45–47, 135–39). The text is not without supernatural elements also. On one central occasion in the novel, Stephen has a vision, which is presented as not simply a hallucination, but a real experience, of his parents' holding a conversation before he is born. He appears to step back into the past, to witness a scene which seems familiar but at which he could not possibly have been present (except as a cluster of cells in his mother's womb). The experience begins with "a touch of fear" caused by the impossible familiarity of a building. "It was happening too quickly. How could he have expectations without memory?" (61). The building is a pub called The Bell. Stephen is tempted to turn away, to "come another time" (62). However, he realizes that "it was not just a place he was being offered, it was a particular day, this day." Slowly he further realizes that the particular strangeness and familiarity of "this particular location had its origins outside his own existence." He sees that what is before him is a "delicate reconstruction of another time," clearly set against the everyday world from which he has come (a change in the foliage and greenery marks this). He has a firm sense that he has really stepped out of his time into another. "Cars passed close by. If he stepped in their path he could not be touched. The day he now inhabited was not the day he had

CHANGE, DYSTOPIA, AND THE WAY OUT

woken into. He was lucid, determined to advance. He was in another time but he was not overwhelmed. He was a dreamer who knows his dream for what it is and, though fearful, lets it unfold out of curiosity" (62–63). In what follows, Stephen approaches the pub window and through it sees his mother, now a "young woman," in conversation with a man. The conversation is clearly important, and he himself becomes a pale face staring through the glass, like a "spirit, suspended between existence and nothingness" waiting for its outcome. Feelings of fear, doom, and rejection fill him as he ultimately backs away and falls mysteriously into a dark void. He feels himself reverting to a fetuslike state, and finally into nothingness—"he had nowhere to go, no moment which could embody him, he was not expected, no destination or time could be named; for a while he moved forward violently, he was immobile, he was hurtling round a fixed point" (66). He wakes up in Julie's cottage on his and her marriage bed.

The remarkable feature of this episode is that it is not presented as a hallucination. Although the novel elsewhere strictly follows the conventions of the realist novel, Stephen's metaphysical experience is left for most of the text simply as that—a metaphysical experience that cannot be explained away. One can contrast here Stephen's vision of Kate in another young girl which is, despite its initial force, presented as an illusion and recognized as such by Stephen himself (165–79). Indeed, the text confirms the actuality of what Stephen has gone through outside The Bell in Mrs. Lewis's account of a conversation she had with her husband-to-be before Stephen was born. His mother is pregnant; she wishes her young man to marry her. He is reluctant, and an abortion appears likely. But glancing out the pub window, Stephen's mother sees, she says, a face, pleading, white, looking in. She is convinced that it is the face of the child she will bear, and decides not to have an abortion (207). After Mrs. Lewis has told her story, Stephen gives his version of what he has seen, which closely matches hers. His mother does not reject anything he tells her. "She spoke only when he had finished, and then it was a brief sigh. 'Ah well. . . .' There was no need for discussion" (209). Thus, in a novel that fundamentally sticks to the laws of the empirical universe, Stephen's supernatural experience is confirmed and validated, and certainly not explained away as hallucination.

The Child in Time is not the generic kaleidoscope that is found in novels by McEwan's contemporaries such as Graham Swift (*Waterland* [1983]) or Timothy Mo (*An Insular Possession* [1986]). However, it does mix genres in a fairly striking manner. Psychological fiction, political-social criticism, dystopia, tutorial on the mysteries of modern physics, and novel with supernatural elements (fitting, in fact, a persuasive definition of the fantastic text)[8]—this is, indeed, a substantial generic range for one text. Psychological and dystopic elements predominate, but the others are strongly, if intermittently, present also.

It is worth asking what the functions of such genre mixture might be. One answer is that genre mixture is simply a remarkably common feature of British fiction in the 1980s and early 1990s.[9] On the other hand, it is reasonable to assume that such a textual feature does have some particular function or functions within a text. This is the case with *The Child in Time*. Genre mixture serves to create a vision of a rich and varied world, in which characters have to live as psychological-emotional, political, and intellectual beings and in which, as is suggested below, healing in one sphere gives hope of healing in another. Also genre mixture, like the text's narrational strategy and specific use of language, helps to remind the reader that different discourses make sense of the world in different ways, and this relativity is strongly echoed in other aspects of the novel discussed below.

One of the differences that critics note between *The Child in Time* and McEwan's earlier fiction is the way in which public life and history are strongly present in the later novel. The principal features of the novel's concern with history have been sketched out in the discussion of socially critical and dystopic elements in the novel. All these embody radical historical changes in the created world of the novel. Licensed begging has been introduced, schools have been sold off to private bidders, the police have been armed (although the last is simply registered as part of the novel's created world rather than as a change, the fact that it is recorded at all suggests it is meant to seem strange to the reader). In terms of historical events, a world war almost breaks out, and the British Government publishes a handbook on childcare that is seen as a cultural landmark (211–14). Stephen feels that he has come close to the inner workings of history as public life in his experience of the whole cynical business of the Child Care Commission and the report (214). And indeed, Stephen does at times come close to the center of politics in his encounters with the prime minister. Singled out for private conversation, invited to lunch, finally forced to meet the prime minister and all her/his panoply of modern power in his own home, Stephen is for a few moments in the presence of one of those who makes history (93–96, 153–54, 180–81, 217–26). The power of his historical guest is made clear when the prime minister's entourage takes over Stephen's apartment with the telephone switchboards, the colored telephones, the secretaries, and the paraphernalia of authority (218–19).

This incident is typical of the way in which Stephen experiences history directly. On two occasions he has abrasive encounters with licensed beggars. Early in the novel a girl beggar singles him out, and Stephen is faced with the dilemma of whether to give and thus tacitly endorse a government policy he abhors or to refuse a request for charity (3–4). This encounter is distressing for Stephen. He resolves his dilemma by giving the girl beggar a five-pound note, whereupon she insults him. Later in the text on his way to see Thelma and Charles, he meets with a group of sturdy beggars outside a hotel. Their mockery of him, and the emotions he feels (bourgeois outrage, guilt), provoke him to reflect on his own past in the hippie 1960s and his own altered and respectable, property-owning state (116–17). His encounters with the prime minister are, above all, personal encounters with the historical, or at least one of the great figures of national history. This is how the prime minister appears to Stephen and his fellow committee members when he/she interrupts their deliberations (93). In this novel, historical change and conditions are a personal matter.

History seems to be a matter of loss in this novel, of radical change which has altered the face of Britain, filling the cities with licensed beggars, causing public transport to collapse, running down educational provision, and transforming the English countryside into a vast conifer plantation. The past (its institutions, its landscapes) has been destroyed in the name of efficiency, individual freedom, and national self-sufficiency. Mr. Lewis's shocked response to the new Britain that he sees in his journey across London captures this aspect of the novel (209). Stephen, given his attitudes toward the prime minister and the Britain that surrounds him, clearly shares his father's feelings.

This motif of historical loss is matched by motifs of a general and widespread loss and transience. This is part of the meaning of "in Time" in the novel's title: time is loss; time is transience. At one point Stephen reflects that what distinguishes men from women is the latter's "faith in endless mutability," a sense that the world, and all within it, is constantly changing and can constantly be altered (59). "Endless mutability" certainly marks the created world of the text. The whole novel centers on the fact of Stephen's and Julie's loss of their daughter, and her constant change and development apart from them ("There was a biological clock, dispassionate in its unstoppability . . ." [2]). But motifs of loss and mutability permeate the rest of the text too. Before he recalls his losing his daughter in the supermarket, Stephen thinks of the landscape outside his old school and how it had been transformed when he revisited it. "And since loss was his subject, it was an easy move to a frozen, sunny day outside a supermarket in South London" (8). It is "the first full flood of understanding of the true nature of his loss" which reduces him to tears in his now empty home (24).

But destruction in time—the annihilation of hope, of ambition, of promise—is widespread throughout the text. For example, Stephen reflects on what has become of his friends from student days, "the aesthetic and political experimenters, the visionary drug-takers" (25). All have "settled for even less" than he has. Harassed and ill-paid teachers, cleaners, taxi drivers, all have failed to fulfill their promise. One is even a licensed beggar. Stephen's first, best-selling children's novel is about transience. "Reading you," says Charles Darke, "they get wind of the idea that they are finite as children" (33). When Stephen visits his parents, he notes their aging, the slipping away of their time together (50). His memories include sitting on an airplane, waiting for it to take off, to carry him away from his parents to boarding school in England. "Stephen was old enough to know that a period of his life, a time of unambiguous affinities, was over. He pressed his face against the window and began to cry. His Brylcreem was all over the glass" (83). His parents, waiting on the tarmac, vanish from view, and Stephen notes that grief for transience is quite general, for the old lady in the seat next to him is crying too (83).

The motif recurs constantly. An expert witness for the Child Care Commission argues that "premature literacy" causes a loss, a "banishment from the Garden" (86). Mr. Lewis muses over "the irretrievable past" (101), and Stephen's encounter with the sturdy beggars makes him reflect on the transformations time has wrought in him (116–17). Stephen's sense of loss continues to overwhelm him at certain moments in the novel: when buying Christmas presents for the daughter he lost years ago (150); when standing in her now empty bedroom (192–93). Toward the end of the novel, Stephen encounters a dying beggar girl, the same one he met in the novel's opening. She and her death become metaphors of the destructive effects of time. "He recognized, beneath the nylon anorak, the yellow frock, now gray. The face, though unmistakable, was transformed. The mocking liveliness was gone. The skin was pock-marked and coarsened, pudgily slack around features which had edged closer together for safety" (228). Soon afterward, he has to deal with his friend Charles's death as well (233). Mutability and the fragility of things in time are constantly emphasized and generalized.

Indeed, the novel to a large extent focuses on attempts to recover what has been lost. There is a constant emphasis on memory.

CHANGE, DYSTOPIA, AND THE WAY OUT

Stephen continually remembers past events while sitting in the childcare committee. Mrs. Lewis recalls her first meeting with her future husband and her later discussion with him concerning her pregnancy. Stephen for considerable parts of the text attempts to find his daughter, to fill the void she has left—through incessant activity, with drink and inane television programs, by buying Kate Christmas presents although he has no way of giving them to her, and finally by loving his wife again and having another child. Charles Darke's regression into childhood can be seen to be an extreme attempt, and finally a failed one, to regain a lost childhood. If it is somehow a fraudulent and slightly ridiculous attempt, Stephen is forced to acknowledge that it is a careful and meticulously researched one. Clothing, the contents of pockets, and speech all show a conscious and radical attempt to reverse the flow of time and to regain (or gain for the first time) a paradisiacal childhood (238–40). The Childcare Handbook itself is an attempt to return to a world of past certainties and authority (212–14). It is an irony, Stephen notes, that the Childcare Handbook with its severe authoritarianism is written by Charles himself, by a man who partly wants to flee that harsh world for one of childhood innocence (238–42).

The personal and the historical are fused in *The Child in Time*. The national political process is marked by change and loss, and this new Britain is experienced very directly by characters, especially Stephen. In addition, the features of national history are paralleled in characters' private lives. This is pointed out by Stephen in his conversation with the prime minister's assistant secretary.

> "I resent what the Prime Minister's been doing in this country all these years. It's a mess, a disgrace."

"Then why did you accept the first time?"
"I was a mess too. Depressed. Now I'm not." (180)

One might risk the suggestion that Stephen's and Julie's experience of loss and their manner of coping with it are meant to parallel the malaise of the novel's Britain. Here, too, transience and loss in time must be dealt with. An unpalatable presence must be lived with and moved beyond. Stephen and Julie's reawakened love and the child that results from it are surely meant to suggest a hope not just for the individual relationships of the text, but also for the country whose unhappiness and misfortune match theirs.

Time is not just connected with loss and possible recovery, but also with relativity. Thelma notes that there is a whole range of explanations of the phenomenon of time, and she holds out the hope that in the future radically different experiences of time—linear, commonsense time, physicists' discussions of time, the time of mystics, dreamers' time, the complex time schemes of novelists—will be somehow unified (135–39). Motifs of relativity abound in the novel. The particularity, specificity, and limitedness of any vision of reality are strongly emphasized from the beginning of the novel. For example, the drivers sitting in their cars in the huge traffic jam which paralyzes London each morning are passed by the commuters walking on the pavements. But that is not how it seems to them. "The steady forward press of the pavement crowds must have conveyed to them a sense of relative motion, of drifting slowly backwards," suggests the narrator (1–2). A few pages later the narrator notes that our perception of time may be faulty: "But time—not necessarily as it is, for who knows that—monomaniacally forbids second chances" (10). As Stephen walks toward Julie's cottage, he notes that "on both sides there were planted lines of conifers with their flashing parallax as one row ceded to the next, a pleasing effect which conveyed a false sense of speed" (55). Here the word "parallax" refers to the relativity of vision, the seeming change in an object's position (among other things) according to the point of view of the observer.

Childcare itself is particularly appropriate to the novel's emphasis on relativity. "And there was no richer field for speculation assertively dressed as fact than childcare," Stephen reflects (89–91). Then he goes on to list for himself the radically differing accounts of what is good for children over a quite extensive paragraph. After one has read this paragraph, the chapter epigraphs, the quotations from The Authorized Childcare Handbook, become ironic, their firm certainty contrasting with the relativism that the text teaches. They become examples of self-deluded accounts/descriptions, quite unaware of the partiality of their own version of things. A similar relativity of account is pointed out when Stephen reflects on contemporary discussions of marital breakdown (156). Thelma's comments on the nature of time also touch on this (135). Stephen's near collision with an upturned lorry in chapter 5, too, becomes a focus for motifs of relativity. "In what followed," the narrator comments, "the rapidity of events was accompanied by the slowing of time" (106). After Stephen has skillfully avoided a serious accident, he himself reflects: "The whole experience had lasted no more than five seconds. Julie would have appreciated what had happened to time, how duration shaped itself round the intensity of the event" (108). Joe the lorry driver is later quite confused about how long he remained trapped in his lorry. "How long was I in there?" he asks Stephen. "Two hours? Three?" Stephen answers: "Ten minutes. Or less" (114). In his silent addresses to Julie, Stephen—according to the narrator—bases his positions "on the unhelpful idea of a final truth, an irrefutable overview amounting to a verdict" which would convince Julie that she is wrong (157). This is striking because in all other matters Stephen accepts that what people see "had a lot to do" with their particular position vis-à-vis the object (157). Stephen himself experiences this directly when he sees his daughter in another girl (165–79). Mrs. Lewis gives an account of certain events between her and her future husband (195–208). Mr. Lewis would almost certainly deny the accuracy of her story (102).

The Child in Time constantly foregrounds the notion of the partiality of any account or description, emphasizing in this way its own limitations as such. It is, thus, connected with history in a second (and older) sense of the word—with history as an account of events and processes, rather than as the events and processes themselves. It also focuses on the possibility of any account (or history) through one of its generic aspects—the dystopic element in the text. Many of the components of the created world of the text emphasize the fictionality of the novel. Things have not quite come to such a pass in the documented extratextual world of late-twentieth-century Britain. The police are not yet generally armed. Licensed begging has not yet been introduced. A world war has not hitherto been threatened by a dispute at an Olympic Games. The weather—remarkable heat, followed by biblical quantities of rain (1, 142–43)—is different from that normally ascribed to the British Isles by nonfictional discussions of the country's climate. Throughout, *The Child in Time* via such features advertises its own status as a work of fiction and raises issues about the reliability of any account, such as it is itself.

The question arises as to how all the features of the text cohere. *The Child in Time* is a very complex and rich text, but it is legitimate to ask what holds it together. If anything does, it is the figure of the child, the other part (besides time) of the novel's title. A particular child is lost; children in general grow up and represent the transience and loss that bedevil our lives in time. But the figure of the child also suggests that unhappy circumstances can be altered, that the world (or at any rate British society) can be redeemed, that loss is real but not necessarily permanent. Julie and Stephen have another child who provides a moment of hope at the novel's end. All the novel's relativistic motifs suggest a salutary caution, a corrective to any easy sentimentality (the birth of a child equals new hope). Charles Darke has tried to reverse time and has lived an absurd fiction. Stephen and Julie, however, have not reversed time, but challenged it by creating a new life to replace the lost one. But through its emphasis on its own fictionality, on the relativity that is so underlined throughout the text, the novel warns the reader against an easy complacency. What he/she has read is only one possibility, only one account of the world.

CHAPTER SIX

Brushes with History (I)
The Innocent

"Well done, Ian McEwan," loudly declares the title of Michael Wood's review of *The Innocent* (1990) in the *London Review of Books*, and the reviewer goes on to write what is largely praise of McEwan's "remarkable new novel." It is, he insists, "a haunting investigation into the varying and troubling possibilities of knowledge. The sheer cleverness of the book is dazzling." This is typical of the novel's reception. George Stade in the *New York Times Review of Books* declares that *The Innocent* shows McEwan to be "an acute psychologist of the ordinary mind," admires the "vividly mocked-up historical setting," and notes how the different elements in the story material are well integrated with each other. Although Julian Symons in the *Times Literary Supplement* disputes this last point, he, too, praises the novel for its unusual development of "the material of a conventional thriller," and he compares it to *The Child in Time*, arguing that both novels attempt to combine a dark vision of the world with a more mature and balanced perspective. Joan Smith in the *New Statesman and Scientist* is, however, unstinting in her praise. "This is far and away Ian McEwan's most mature work. . . . *The Innocent* is an outstanding achievement." This view is echoed by no less a figure than Anthony Burgess. "The resonance twangs long after the reading, and this must be the mark of a good novel."[1]

Both Burgess and Symons note the closeness of *The Innocent* to the materials and conventions of popular fiction, specifically to those of the espionage novel, and there is good reason for these observations. The protagonist of the novel, Leonard Markham, is an inexperienced twenty-five-year-old British Post Office engineer who is sent to Berlin in 1955 to work in a joint British and U.S. Intelligence operation (the historically documented "Operation Gold") to dig a tunnel into the territory of the German Democratic Republic in order to tap Soviet and East German military telephone lines. Although he is involved in a lowly capacity (largely to do with testing tape-recording equipment), Leonard observes the whole thing at first hand. His stay in Berlin exposes him to a wide range of new experiences. Leonard has never lived in a foreign city before, and in this case it is Berlin, a city still full of ruins, awash with spies, and, although not yet cut in two by the Wall, divided into mutually hostile zones. In addition, Leonard meets his first Americans here and has to come to terms with the tensions between his English diffidence and the very different natures of the Americans around him, especially that of his superior, the abrasive Glass. Leonard also falls in love in Berlin, and with a slightly older German woman. His affair with Maria leads to a sexual and emotional initiation and maturity for Leonard.

Unfortunately, his relationship with Maria also leads to macabre and appalling violence and misfortune. Maria's ex-husband, the drunken Otto, attacks the young couple on the night of their engagement party, and in the ensuing struggle Otto is killed. Instead of going to the police, Maria and Leonard decide to cut up and dispose of the body. How they do so and how this interweaves with the matter of the tunnel form the latter sections of the novel. Leonard eventually hides the body in the tunnel and then betrays the operation to the Soviets (in fact, it turns out that his betrayal is of little importance, as the Russians and the East Germans knew of the tunnel's existence already). Under the pressure of the awful thing they have done, Maria and Leonard's love withers and breaks down altogether once Leonard is recalled to London. In a Postscript to the novel, Leonard returns to Berlin in mid-1987, a recent letter from Maria in his pocket, revisits the sites of his youthful experiences, and decides to fly to his former lover in her home in the U.S. (she married the American Glass after her affair with Leonard ended).

McEwan's novels have never been marked by complicated narrative organization. They largely proceed in a linear, chronological fashion, and this is the case, too, with *The Innocent*. However, the chapters on *The Cement Garden* and *The Comfort of Strangers* have noted how, on the level of narration (that is, of the voice that tells the story of those novels), there are certain problems, which function to draw attention to the act of narration in a self-referential manner. But as his output grows, narration seems to become progressively a less complex element in McEwan's fiction. Any self-referential element in narration is fairly slim in *The Child in Time*, while in *The Innocent* fictionality seems hardly stressed at all by narrational technique. What is striking, rather, is the genuine traditionality of the technique employed in this text. There is a traditional omniscient narrator throughout the text, commenting in propria persona on the course of events and switching point of view in an unproblematic fashion between the principal characters Leonard and Maria (although Leonard's point of view predominates).

Thus, when Leonard meets Maria for the first time the narrator comments: "He thought, correctly as it turned out, that his life was about to change."[2] In the chapter that follows, the narrator provides a brief sketch of Maria's life and circumstances (47–48). That this is not a representation of Leonard's consciousness or of what he hears in his first conversation with Maria is obvious in the following paragraph. The account of Maria's family's past, her living conditions, and her job has clearly been a narratorial intervention. "A few of these facts Leonard came by after he had stirred himself to move his chair. . . . The rest were accumulated slowly and with difficulty over many weeks" (48). Further passages concerning Maria also involve a narratorial rather than a character point of view. "Many years later," the reader is told, "Leonard had no difficulty at all recalling Maria's face" (53). It is hard to decide whether the description that follows is Leonard's or the narrator's. But a passage such as "The hair itself was peculiarly fine, like a baby's, and often wriggled free of the childish clasps women wore then" (54) is probably delivered by the narrator directly (especially the historical detail of "[which] women wore then"). This is surely true, too, of a passage such as: "It was the sort of face, the sort of manner, onto which men were likely to project their own requirements. One could read womanly power into her silent abstraction, or find a childlike dependency in her quiet attentiveness" (54).

Within this quasi-omniscient narration, the deployment of character point of view is quite consistent. The narrator is able to move into Leonard's or Maria's consciousness quite seamlessly and easily. For example, Leonard reflects: "He should do without his glasses. The things he really wanted to see were up close. A circuit diagram, a valve filament, another face. A girl's face" (5). This is part of an interior monologue represented by free indirect speech/thought. The same is true of a subsequent passage concerning Maria. "She stood close so he could see her clearly. How wonderful it was, not to be frightened of a man" (67). This is typical of the novel as a whole. The focus is predominantly on Leonard's point of view, but the narrator persistently gives Maria's, too, and the whole technique is consistent throughout the text.

Just as narration in *The Innocent* seems markedly less a self-referential device than in McEwan's previous novels, so, too, language draws attention to itself and thus to the storytelling act to a much lesser degree. There are sections where the text's language is clearly foregrounded, although these are isolated fragments and this foregrounding of language does not seem to permeate the text as a whole. But foregrounding of language there is, largely through a formality of style. For example, when Leonard sits in a Berlin bar for the first time, he has difficulty understanding the conversations going on around him. "At first he heard only the seamless, enfolded intricacies of vowels and syllables, the compelling broken rhythms, the delayed fruition of German sentences" (7). Here the formality of "seamless, enfolded intricacies" and "delayed fruition" stand out, particularly as they are not part of Leonard's own vocabulary. The same is true a little later when Leonard observes two U.S. Army sergeants practicing American football. Here the narrator talks of "the jubilant uncoiling power that made the orange ball soar," of "the parabolic symmetry of its rise and fall," and of "an unforced subversion of the surroundings" (18). Again, these are not Leonard's words (it does not sound like anything he says or thinks anywhere in the novel), and their formality stands in marked contrast both to the rest of the vocabulary surrounding them and to the subject which they are describing (two men throwing a ball to one another).

But such self-advertising style is rare in *The Innocent*. Much more prominent is a rather different vocabulary and syntax which at no point seem to be drawing attention to themselves, an accessible style which focuses the reader's attention primarily on the subject of the discourse and not on the language itself. It surely takes some effort on the reader's part to concentrate on language in the following passage. "They turned down a narrower road which tapered off into a track. Off to the left was a newly surfaced road. Glass tilted his head back and indicated with his beard. Two hundred yards ahead, obscured at first by the stark forms of an orchard that lay behind it, was their destination. It resolved itself into two principal buildings. One was two storeys high and had a gently pitched roof, the other, which ran off from the first at an angle, was low and gray, like a cell block. The windows, which formed a single line, appeared to be bricked in" (15). Examples of similar passages may be found throughout the text. If it be objected that such a style is appropriate to the description of buildings or of mechanical processes, then one could point to a number of highly emotional passages where the style is similarly configured, for example, the passage at the start of chapter 17, just after Maria and Leonard have killed Otto (179–80). Here sentences are relatively short (at times they are mere phrases) and the vocabulary is largely simple and neutral. The same is true of the section of the text that describes Leonard and Maria's dismemberment of Otto (195–205). Apart from occasional slightly formal phrases (such as "exposing the vivid mess of Otto's digestive tract" or "disgorged" [203]), the style is predominantly an anonymous and neutral one. Simple and compound sentences predominate, and there is little syntactical complexity. Vocabulary is accessible and relatively unremarkable. Examples of this latter style abound in *The Innocent*. Unlike in McEwan's earlier novels, it is not used to draw attention to the text itself and the act of storytelling. In *The Innocent* the focus is firmly on the story material itself, much less on the means by which it is presented.

Reviewers of *The Innocent* comment on the psychological aspects of the novel and on its use of the traditional motifs and settings of espionage fiction.[3] This clearly points to an element of genre mixture within the text. It should come as no surprise that *The Innocent* is marked by genre mixture, as this is such a recurrent (almost a defining) feature of late-twentieth-century British fiction. Most clearly the text oscillates between being a psychological novel—a study of a crucial experience in a young man's life, and an analysis of the circumstances within which two essentially decent and humane people (innocents) can commit the most brutal of crimes—and a piece of espionage fiction. The psychological aspect of the novel is clear throughout, for example, when it focuses on Leonard's discovery of sexual pleasure (70). Other passages representing the psychological focus of the novel are the crucial chapters 17 and 18 that present the psychological results of Maria and Leonard's situation in a very direct manner. The anguished italics of chapter 17 do this, as does the movement into free indirect thought in chapter 18 (200). Other examples are Leonard's self-scrutiny and self-justification in chapter 21 (241–42) or his complex feelings about Maria as he leaves Berlin (ch. 22).

The Innocent is also a piece of espionage fiction. This aspect of the text is very prominent. The Berlin setting; the emphasis on the divided nature of the city; one of the central actions of the novel, the building of a tunnel into East Germany in order to tap Soviet military communications; the cameo appearance of a nonfictional spy (George Blake); the relatively complex plot (Blake has long ago betrayed the tunnel, but the final breaking into it occurs because he informs his masters of the supposed presence of special decoding devices there, which, in fact, are Leonard's suitcases full of Otto's dismembered body)—all these function as very clear genre-markers. Espionage-novel elements form a continuous backdrop to the psychological aspects. For example, there is the rigmarole about "levels" and "clearance" (16), an element that will later play an important, if comic, role in the novel's plot.

The landscape, too, is clearly a cold war Berlin recognizable from dozens of novels and films (see, for example, chapter 2 [19]), and *The Innocent* alludes directly to the popular novels of John le Carré and Len Deighton, novels that in many ways achieve the apogee of their complexity and sophistication in the 1980s. (*A Perfect Spy* [1986] by le Carré and *Berlin Game* [1984] by Deighton are examples which readily spring to mind.) However, there is certainly a difference between a John le Carré novel, let alone a Len Deighton one, and *The Innocent*. While highly sophisticated espionage fiction like the novels mentioned above is also marked by genre mixture, the balance between (or among) genres is rather different. In *A Perfect Spy*, for instance, the espionage novel element is fundamental, the psychological novel element secondary. (This is even more true of Deighton's novels.) In *The Innocent*, matters are the other way around. It is fundamentally a psychological novel (a story of love and crime and their emotional consequences) for which the espionage elements are primarily a backdrop (although a highly integrated one).

The function of genre mixture in le Carré's and Deighton's novels is also different from that in *The Innocent*. In the former its function is, above all, to ennoble and elevate a popular genre by fusing with it a hierarchically higher genre (for example, the psychological novel or the historical novel). In McEwan's novel, genre mixture has the kind of self-referential function it does elsewhere in his fiction and in that of others of his generation. The fusion of two genres, especially since one of them is essentially formulaic (the espionage novel), surely draws attention to the fictional act. It reminds the reader of the text's status as text, particularly by drawing in elements (those of espionage fiction) that by the late 1980s have almost a clichéd aspect to them.

The Innocent has another kind of intertextual reference as well, that is, to its own contemporary literary environment. It can be seen as an almost schematic gathering of certain motifs and concerns of the novelists of McEwan's own generation. It does this through its focus on abroad, on what is not British and what is clearly differentiated from it. In the novel this has both a German and an American aspect. Certainly, motifs of the foreign and what it means to Leonard are recurrent throughout the text. "Perhaps I just like to be abroad," Leonard declares toward the end of the novel (231), and constantly Berlin and being out of England are felt to be much more interesting, much more exciting than being in England. Leonard's excitement is palpable as he walks about the still bomb-damaged Berlin (5–6). He is both fascinated and irritated, but predominantly fascinated, by the U.S. Army sergeants playing American football (17–18) and enthralled by the un-English quantities of food available in the staff canteen (25).

But it is primarily in his relationship with Maria that Leonard feels the difference between home and abroad and in which he feels a liberation, an escape into newness and excitement, for example, when he contrasts her room with his parents' house in Tottenham

(61–62). The change that Maria's room brings him, its foreignness, its separateness from all that England and his inhibited, middle-class past stands for, is very clear. "Sitting in the darkening, chilly room in his raincoat, holding on to her hand, he felt he was throwing away his life. The abandonment was delicious" (64). "In this bare little room with its pile of assorted shoes belonging to a woman who lived alone and did not fuss with milk jugs or doilies on tea trays, it should have been possible to deal in unadorned truths" (65). Maria's foreignness, her being German, adds to her attraction. "He liked speaking German, he was even getting good with her encouragement, and he preferred Berlin to any place he had ever been" (146). American music starts to enthrall him. He finds it exciting, but it has a further attraction. "Beyond the excitement Leonard took satisfaction in dancing in a way his parents and their friends did not, and could not, and in liking music they would hate, and in feeling at home in a city where they would never come. He was free" (150). The contrast between home and abroad, and Leonard's love of the latter, is made very prominent during Leonard's return to England at Christmas. The difference is between freedom, excitement, and being in touch with world-historical events, on one hand, and being mired in provincial and drab triviality, on the other (139–41). Here the contrast between a desperately dull and trivial England and an exciting and dynamic abroad is very marked. Berlin is the site of Leonard's alteration and his freedom.

This cosmopolitanism is something that recurs in a number of McEwan's novels (*The Comfort of Strangers* and *Black Dogs*, as well as *The Innocent*) and is, furthermore, a tendency that shows no signs of abating in the 1990s. Thus, McEwan's *The Innocent* stands in an almost paradigmatic relationship to much of the British fiction

surrounding it, at the end of the decade summing up a particular tendency within that fiction and also pointing toward future developments. To some extent it is a novel about the liberations that abroad
brings, not just to its characters, but to fiction itself.

But *The Innocent* is, above all, about a brush with history. In
her letter, written to Leonard long after the events of 1955 and 1956,
Maria Eckdorf, now Glass, writes: "We all have to make our own
arrangements with the past" (262). This sentence, and indeed her
whole letter, embodies the concern of *The Innocent* with history in
the double sense noted earlier with regard to *The Child in Time*—
that is, with history as event and process and with history as account.
The Innocent is a novel deeply imbued with historical elements and
prominently concerned with the problems of giving an account of
events. Similarly, Maria in her letter has to give an account of past
events, caught up with the historically significant, and shows herself
aware of the problematic nature of any such account, any such
"accommodation."

The historical, as event and process, permeates *The Innocent*.
First, it is a novel that provides clear dates to localize its action. The
workers' uprising of 1953 in East Berlin is used to do this (36), as is
the building of the Wall in 1961 (257); elsewhere quite precise dates
are given (131, 149, 262). Second, the protagonists live through or
live with the consequences of certain major historical events and
processes. This has both a German and a U.S. dimension. In a sense,
it hardly has a British dimension at all, inasmuch as specifically
British history is barely alluded to, but it is important to emphasize
that it is Leonard, a young Englishman, who is encountering and
experiencing historical change.

History has a U.S. dimension, too, in the novel. Glass's friend Russell also has his memories of the end of the war and of the early days of the cold war (39–40). The whole action of the novel, indeed, is closely bound up with the cold war—its espionage, its hostilities, its landscape. Operation Gold (the tunnel) is like a battle in other wars. However, it is on the process of U.S. domination of the cultural sphere that the novel, through Leonard, particularly dwells. Even before he meets Glass, Leonard "had an intimation of the power of American style" (8). His own clothes, his own Englishness seem already shabby and feeble in comparison with the forcefulness of the American he has not yet even met. Once he encounters Glass, Leonard is indeed struck by energy and force (9–10). When Leonard speaks to Glass, he begins to alter. "His [Leonard's] voice sounded prissy in his ears. In deference to Glass, he was softening his 't's' and flattening his 'a's'"(10). Leonard, too, is both repelled and fascinated by the sight of two U.S. Army sergeants practicing American football throws. The casual elegance and power, the subversion of British standards enthralls him. "This was a blatant exhibition of physical prowess. These were grown men, showing off;" "This was all swank, childishness" (18). American music and American radio, and all that they imply about U.S. power and cultural presence, provide a background to Leonard and Maria's affair (132). A later passage also dwells on the excitements, the freedoms, the enthralling rebelliousness which U.S. music allows Leonard to feel in early 1956 (149–50). This whole process is not without tensions for Leonard. At one point, Glass's patronizing authority provokes the Englishman to speak out. Notably, he does so in (mildly) nationalist terms (135). Operation Gold is a historical event in a sequence of historical events (the cold war), and the power relations within that operation represent a historical process. They embody an American hegemony in European affairs.

The Innocent is also concerned with history as account. (As indicated in the previous chapter, this is a closely related, and older, meaning of the word "history".) There are frequent references to stories of varying kinds throughout the text. "Yeah, there's a story behind that. I'll tell you later," Glass promises Leonard (20). Leonard eavesdrops on "stories" at other tables in the canteen (72–73). The narrator gives them at least in part, and then adds another about the head of the Berlin CIA base (74–75). Glass constructs a story around Maria's disappearance which demands that he investigate her absence (108). In the immediate aftermath of Otto's death, Leonard reflects that "He needed a sequence, a story. He needed order" (179). A little later, while he and Maria are reviewing their options, he says: ". . . we have done nothing wrong, we have to make them believe it, we have to get our story right" (186). In her letter to Leonard, Maria tells him a story about past events, and within that she uses the phrase "the whole story" about her confession to Glass (263–64).

The motif of story merges into that of fiction. The matter of the different "levels" of information and initiation within the warehouse and the tunnel project has to do with story and fiction. Each person at each level is told a story that will keep him satisfied until he finds there is another story and that what he has is partly fiction. "Everybody thinks his clearance is the highest there is, everyone thinks he has the final story. You only hear of a higher level at the moment you're being told about it" (16). Even something as trivial as a shopping list can become a text which creates a fiction. The list Leonard prepares creates a specific, quite false image of its author. "He read the list through as he stood. He felt himself to be precisely what his list suggested: unencumbered, manly, serious" (29–30). The bland letters he writes to his parents are also fictions (112). Leonard's violent sexual fantasies are expressed as an indulgence in fictional images of himself. "There were figures gathering at the edge of thought, now they were striding towards the center, towards him. They were all versions of himself, and he knew he could not resist them. . . . They were alien to his obliging and kindly nature" (92–93). During their love-making, when he fantasizes about his domination of Maria and about her responses, he is indulging in a fiction (94). The whole tunnel and its buildings are a fiction, seemingly a warehouse, aimed at the watching East Germans. George Blake is an English officer who is in fact a Soviet spy.

Motifs of interpretation and misinterpretation are also frequent. This has a comic dimension. In the bar on his first evening in Berlin, Leonard overhears what he is convinced is an argument about genocide, justified war crimes, and brutality (7–8). What else would a conversation in German with words like "train," "death," and "bring" entail? Later when his German is better, Leonard realizes that he is listening to quite normal everyday pub conversations (112). The story of Bill Harvey and George is similarly one of comic misinterpretation. George is not a soldier, it turns out, but a dog (74–75). Glass's reordering of the facts of Maria's return to her parents produces a radical misinterpretation of her actions. She is not a Russian agent, but rather an offended lover (108).

The created world of *The Innocent* is full of lies and misinterpretations. It seems that finding a true account of events is remarkably difficult. The problem of history in the sense of narrative account

is, thus, underlined throughout the novel. In this respect, *The Innocent* shows certain clear similarities with *The Child in Time*, where
historical events and the problems of giving an account of them are
a central focus. In its concern with the problematic nature of any
narrative, *The Innocent* also echoes the self-referential function of
narrational complexity and formality of language in *The Cement
Garden* and *The Comfort of Strangers*, novels in which the author
goes out of his way to remind the reader of the narrational act and
its linguistic substance (and, thus, its limitedness and partiality).
However, *The Innocent* does also differ radically in this matter from
its predecessors. In the earlier novels, fictionality is stressed at all
levels, including narration and language. In *The Innocent*, this is
hardly the case at all. The novel's metafictional elements, its foregrounded emphasis on its own fictionality, exist primarily on the
level of genre and intertextuality and of motif. Here their presence
is marked, but they are not supported by all aspects of the text.
While they are prominent, they seem overshadowed by the pattern
of motifs of innocence and maturity, of innocence and corruption.
This seems to mark a movement in McEwan's fiction away from
metafictional concerns toward the psychological ones that have
always filled his novels and short stories, and toward a more socially
and morally didactic stance.

In *The New York Times Book Review*, Stade praises McEwan
as "an acute psychologist of the ordinary mind" and admires his
"tunneling operation into the cesspits of ordinary minds."[4] *The Innocent*, indeed, does take the form of a psychological study, principally
of its central character, Leonard. This is clearly signaled on a number of occasions—in passages which focus on Leonard's emotions
("His heart was a ratchet, with each thud he was wound tight,

harder" [51]); on recollection and introspection ("Many years later, Leonard had no difficulty at all recalling Maria's face" [53]); on fantasy ("Yes, she was defeated, conquered, his by right, could not escape, and now, *he was a soldier*, weary, battle-marked and bloody" [94]); and on hallucinations ("He was seeing objects drifting on the periphery of vision: an English letter box, a stag with high antlers, a table-lamp. When he turned to them they dissolved" [211]). Evidently this is a novel aiming to provide a psychological portrait, a picture of the movements of a particular mind. And *The Innocent* does depict closely Leonard's psychological development in Berlin, or, if not his development, at least the changes that take place in his character. This is a movement from inexperience and naïveté to something that is different.

Leonard's inexperience is stressed at the novel's start. He does not know how to deal with Glass's abrasiveness; he has never received an insult since becoming an adult (27); he is not used to the self-dramatizing of adult Americans (50). When he receives a note from Maria at a night-club, he responds as a child, fearing for a moment it is from his mother (44), and a trip back home to his parents' house in a London suburb can return him rapidly to the position of a child (142–43). As he tends Maria, beaten up by her ex-husband Otto, he reflects on how little he knows about people and what they are capable of (137). "Why am I so ignorant?" he exclaims at one point to Maria, to which she replies: "Not ignorant. Innocent" (158). It is this innocence, this näiveté that is dismantled in the course of the novel, though whether this dismantling is an improvement is open to question.

Berlin certainly changes Leonard. After a few weeks in the city, his previous self-confident pride in its destruction during the war seems "puerile, repellent" to him (56). His affair with Maria is an initiation into knowledge of a woman, of sex, of kinds of physical and emotional experiences he has never enjoyed before (63–64, 68). Maria still calls him "*Mein Dummerchen*, my little innocent" as he explores her body (89), but he has gained enormously in experience with her. The relationship with Maria brings him to serious emotions (he has never had one before, he feels) (120–21), and to expression of them, in a way that he could never have achieved previously (125–26). It brings him (and Maria) an extraordinary sense of freedom from the restrictions of their past lives and even, in its early stages, from all social norms (132–33). The day-to-day routines of their life together make Leonard feel "grown-up at last" and even "civilized" (133, 157). But the movement from innocence also brings with it darker experiences—rape fantasies (92), violent hatred and jealousy of Glass (108), and finally the plunge into an abyss of violence and horror in the murder of Otto and his dismemberment (chs. 16–18). Yet, at the end of it all, Leonard remains, in a certain sense, still innocent. He certainly asserts his lack of guilt. As the U.S. guards make to open the case containing Otto's cut-up body, Leonard reflects: "He had done his best, and he knew he was not a particularly bad person" (226). Later he makes in his imagination a long speech, trying to explain his actions and their causes, trying to deny his guilt (241–42). "He was innocent," he thinks to himself, "that he knew" (241). The novel leaves it to the reader to decide. Is the gain in experience worth the loss of innocence? Does experience always carry with it the potential for horror? In what sense does Leonard (and Maria too) remain innocent (guiltless? naive?) after his terrible crime?

But, certainly, Maria and Leonard are surrounded by innocents. The soldiers guarding the warehouse above the tunnel know nothing, Glass tells Leonard (17), and the whole business of different "levels" of knowledge is based on degrees of innocence, in the sense of lack of initiation (16–17). The British scientist MacNamee is childlike, still sporting his milk teeth (79), while Glass sees him as an unreliable little boy who should be playing with a train-set (135). The tunnel itself appears to Leonard as a kind of boyish "toytown" (80), and the whole enterprise of stealing secrets from under the noses of the Russians and the East Germans also seems to him to have something of a children's game about it (141). Americans strike the Englishman as childish: softball reminds him of a British game for children (115); their music and dancing fascinates and repels in its childish freedom from British restraint (115–16, 149–50). Maria distrusts Glass. "His mind is too simple and too busy," she says, as if he were somehow childlike (158). The English are, in fact, not much better. When Leonard goes home for Christmas, the innocent insularity of a Tottenham that knows nothing of the cold war or of the realities of Berlin seems naive (140–41). Even Maria, Leonard's accomplice in crime, when she leaves him at Tempelhof airport, wears a new clasp in her hair, making her look "more childish than ever" (250–51).

However, what *The Innocent* demonstrates is how easy it is for innocents to step into wickedness. This is what Wood refers to when he writes that McEwan specializes in "the Gothic of everyday life."[5] As in *The Comfort of Strangers*, it seems very easy in *The Innocent* to fall into an abyss of horror; a moment's inattention, a wrong turning, not being quite careful enough, bad luck suffice. Leonard has a foretaste of this after he tries to turn his violent sexual fantasies into reality with Maria. He reflects that at the time there seemed "some logic, some crazed, step-by-step reasoning" that brings him to attempt a mock-rape on his lover (105). But this realization comes with full force just after Leonard has cut Otto's torso in two. "There was a moment before he left the room when Leonard suddenly had the measure of the distance they had traveled, the trajectory that had delivered them from their successful little engagement party to this, and how all along the way each successive step had seemed logical enough, consistent with the one before, and how no one was to blame" (203–4). Critics have commented that there is an appropriateness in the novel's setting to this step-by-step lapse into horror. Berlin and Germany immediately call up the question of war-guilt, of the unimaginable (or all too imaginable) atrocities committed by ordinary citizens during the years 1939 to 1945. Smith notes that Otto's dismemberment "recalls the slaughterhouses of the war," and Wood remarks that Leonard's attitude toward his actions recalls German attitudes toward crimes committed during World War II.[6] The narrator, punning, with dark wit, on the metaphor of "having baggage from the past," points to this connection when he has Leonard register that he does not stand out in Berlin with his heavy cases full of body parts, for "Berlin was full of people with heavy luggage" (208).

In *The Cement Garden* and *The Comfort of Strangers*, there is a strong suggestion that male aggression is to blame for much that goes wrong in the world, and this argument is further advanced in *The Innocent*. Certainly, the novel is full of motifs of maleness which are held up to critical scrutiny. Glass is almost a parody of male incisiveness, with his bristling beard, his physical energy, and his knowingness (9–10). The tunnel is not just a boyish game made substantial, but a place inhabited only by men and marked by "a certain virile cult of competence" (21). Leonard's night out with Glass and Russell makes him feel one of a party of responsible and knowledgeable men (38). He is stirred by the "virile insistence" of the song "Rock Around the Clock" (116), while his downstairs neighbor, the covert spy George Blake, is, like Glass, a model (almost a comic one) of male competence and aggression (122–23). The novel shows Leonard accommodating himself to this model of maleness. At first this is comic. He fills out a shopping list, and this makes him feel "manly, serious" (30). Later, however, his fantasies of male domination over women culminate in his absurd attempt to rape his lover (92–98). Later still, he imagines dealing with Otto in all kinds of clinically violent ways; none of his fantasies, however, approximate the awful reality of his fight with Maria's ex-husband (144, 173–77). Maria, too, has complex attitudes toward male aggression. She has a memory of a wartime rape (98–99), and it is Leonard's vulnerability and lack of aggression that appeal to her (67). She scolds Leonard in her letter for being "so male" in withdrawing into anger and silence after their love turns sour (267). Yet, in extremis, faced with Otto's violence and Leonard's perverse jealousy, she helps to precipitate the fight by shouting, "You're a man, throw him out!" (170).

The Innocent is an accomplished novel. It takes the material of a popular genre and mixes it with concerns from serious fiction. It charts an encounter with history and experience, and is a fascinating study of innocence and guilt and male responsibility for the darker side of things. Its concern with questions of knowledge and of the historical account is cleverly integrated into the whole text. For the reader of McEwan's fiction, it also marks an interesting tendency in his work, one that is already evident in *The Child in Time:* that is, a movement away from metafictional concerns. The interest in questions of knowledge, which are part of McEwan's (and any other writer's) metafictional interests, is still there, but this is embodied on the level of topic only rather than in technical aspects of the text. This is a movement that will become even more marked in two of McEwan's subsequent novels, *Black Dogs* and *Enduring Love.*

CHAPTER SEVEN

Brushes with History (II)
Black Dogs

"A Goodbye to Gore" is the title of Andrew Billen's interview with McEwan, published to coincide with the *Observer*'s review of *Black Dogs*.[1] This time, for sure, the story material of McEwan's novel seems to lack the grisly horrors of his earlier fiction. No incest, no sadistic slaughter, no child kidnapping, no dismemberment of dead bodies—*Black Dogs* (1992) is the story of a family disagreement. This short novel (around 150 to170 pages in different editions) is narrated by Jeremy, middle-aged, bland, happily married and successful after an unhappy, orphaned, isolated youth and drifting, rootless adulthood. Having married into the Tremaine family, he becomes fascinated by his wife's parents, Bernard and June, by their romance in the mid-1940s, by their marriage and its subsequent disruption in 1946, and by the nature of and reasons for their long forty-year estrangement. In 1946, June has a vision of the divine that leads her to abandon the left-wing politics she has hitherto shared with her husband and to become a mystic recluse. Bernard remains loyal to his rationality, his belief in the authority of science, and his first Communist and then Labour Party politics. They live a life of peculiar estrangement, she in France, he in London, unable to part or be reconciled.

In the mid- to late-1980s, Jeremy, undecided, questioning, and longing for substitute parents, tries to understand their different philosophical positions while also attempting to unravel the circumstances of the event that led to June's adoption of a metaphysical understanding of the world. This incident gives the novel its title. While hiking in Southern France in 1946, June is attacked by two huge black dogs that for her seem to incarnate a terrible evil at the heart of the universe. In a moment of revelation, however, as the beasts close in, she discovers a sense of the divine within her that allows her to resist these hellhounds.

In keeping with its narrational frame—Jeremy is trying to write a memoir of his parents-in-law—the novel's action moves backward and forward between settings in the late-1980s and the mid-1940s. It also moves around Europe: various sections take place in an English nursing home, in Southern France, in Poland, and in Berlin in November 1989 when the Berlin Wall begins to be dismantled. For such a short text, *Black Dogs* strikes one immediately as remarkably ambitious. Within the framework of a family dispute, it attempts to touch upon the clash of science and mysticism, rationality and magic, violence and love, and civilization and its abandonment. Within that same framework, it also delves into some of the major currents and events of late-twentieth-century European history: the legacy of World War II, the German death camps of the 1940s, the promises and failures of Soviet Communism, the axial moment of the fall of the Berlin Wall in 1989. Toward the end of the text, one is aware of the European focus of the novel's action. Bernard has a vision of Europe terminally polluted by the brutalities of its mid-twentieth-century bloodletting (140), and Jeremy concludes with his visionary warning that the black dogs will return at some other time in Europe (148–49). For such a short novel about a family quarrel, *Black Dogs* covers a wide range of material.

Its reception was, to say the least, mixed. "This formidable novel is McEwan's best yet," declares an anonymous reviewer in the *Observer*, and this judgment is echoed by Andrew Billen in an earlier interview/review of the novel. In the *London Review of Books*, Graham Coster makes comparisons of the novel to E. M. Forster's work, and in a later review of McEwan's *Enduring Love*, Michael Wood draws parallels between *Black Dogs* and Golding's novels (in both cases, high praise indeed). Caroline Moore in the *Spectator* declares: "This is not McEwan's best book (though *The Child in Time* is so good that this is praising with faint damns)." M. John Harrison in the *Times Literary Supplement*, on the other hand, does not mince words: "McEwan's retreat from the cement garden of his earlier books has been exemplary. Human beings are 'just animals with clothes on,' claims the narrator of 'Last Day of Summer' (*First Love, Last Rites*, 1976). *Black Dogs*, made from kindlier assumptions, is a complex statement about violence, that 'disease of the human imagination.' It is compassionate without resorting to sentimentality, clever without losing its honesty, an undisguised novel of ideas which is also Ian McEwan's most human work." These are the terms in which critics express their approval of the novel—the usual increased maturity that reviewers like to observe in McEwan's work, a greater compassion for his characters, a willingness to tackle big ideas—coupled with an appreciation of the skill with which his narrative is assembled (as the poet Craig Raine remarks, it is "a novel whose formal perfection was so subtle that most critics failed to notice").[2]

But even positive reviews contain criticisms. Coster finds the concluding section of the novel inconsistent with the rest. He argues that an authoritative narrative is offered in this final part, while earlier sections have demonstrated that no such thing is possible. Even Wood has hesitations in his comparison with Golding. Both McEwan and Golding write philosophical parables, he argues, and are thus engaged in "rather awkward work. . . . The awkward work is that of directed thinking, which has always been difficult for the novel." There are also several quite negative reviews. For example, James Saynor in the *Observer* calls *Black Dogs* "such a wan and fractured disappointment" with "forced" imagery and "schematic characterization." In the *Literary Review* Amanda Craig dismisses the novel. "What could have been made into a pleasing essay on the ambiguous nature of memory and desire, or the real and the ideal, gets lost in portentous . . . polemic," she insists. This critic also finds that the novel's implication that the male black dog has been trained by the Nazis to rape women drags the text "into farce."

Where does *Black Dogs* stand in relation to McEwan's earlier fiction? In certain respects the novel seems to mark a further step away from the technically problematic and problematizing aspects of the previous novels. This is evident, above all, in terms of the text's narration, language, and genre makeup.

In comparison to *The Cement Garden*, *The Comfort of Strangers*, and *The Child in Time*, *Black Dogs* possesses few, if any, narrational complexities. This, McEwan's fifth novel, continues a movement toward the traditional and the relatively unproblematic in the sphere of narration that began in *The Innocent*. *Black Dogs* is a first-person narration given by Jeremy, the son-in-law of the Tremaines, whose lives and disputes form the central focus of the novel. It is presented as a "memoir," and the circumstances of its composition are given and clearly established.[3] The Preface, with its dedication, its apology to the family, its circumstantial detail, aims at a strong degree of verisimilitude. One is constantly reminded of Jeremy's notebook, his transcribing of memories (xxiv, 9, 26, 29, 38, 147). The narration is unified and thoroughly verisimilar (that is, it aims to look probable and likely). Jeremy's voice is consistent throughout; where he is not present at certain events, he carefully explains the source of his knowledge (usually the reminiscences of June and Bernard, his parents-in-law). "She tilted her head back and closed her eyes, her posture for delving at length. We had been over this more than once before, how and why June had changed her life" (16). "I once asked Bernard about his first meeting with June during the war. What drew him to her? He remembered no first encounter" (23). But this explanation is not always necessary. Frequently Jeremy himself is witness to and participant in many of the events narrated, for example, the section set in Berlin in 1989 (part 2), or that in the hotel in St. Maurice de Navacelles (part 3).

Just as narration scarcely draws attention to itself in *Black Dogs*, so the language of the text is not foregrounded as it so clearly is in McEwan's first three novels. Here, too, as in narration, one can note a withdrawal from the self-referential and problematic toward the transparent and reticent. There are certainly passages of some syntactic and lexical complexity in *Black Dogs*. For example, in his Preface, Jeremy writes of his liking for his friends' parents and of those friends' contrasting distaste for their parents (xvii-xviii). In these pages, sophistication is evident in vocabulary—Jeremy uses phrases like "a masochistic lunge at downward social mobility" (of his friends), "the leather feticheur" and "tuberous forearms" (of his sister's boyfriend), or "the symmetry of our respective disaffections" (of his friends again)—and in syntax: one fifteen-line paragraph (on pages xvii-xviii) consists of one highly complex sentence. But although one might suggest other similar passages (14–15, 122–23, 140), these are not the norm in this novel. Jeremy's language

is educated and relatively sophisticated, but one has little sense of
the self-advertising, stylistic fireworks that one can note in the novels of McEwan's contemporaries like Angela Carter, Graham Swift,
or Timothy Mo, and to some extent even in Kazuo Ishiguro's fiction. Nor indeed are there the passages of remarkable linguistic elab-
oration that one can note in other contemporary novelists. In *Black
Dogs*, the norm is much more one of an unobtrusively educated
vocabulary and syntax, interspersed with occasional formalities. For
example, when Jeremy returns to June's French farmhouse, he
reflects on her presence there even after death (91–92). In this passage, phrases like "the contemplation of eternity" or "some delicate
emanation, a gossamer web of consciousness inhered" stand out in
terms of formality and sophistication, but lexis is predominantly
toward a neutral point on an informality-formality scale. The same
is true of syntax; complexity when it occurs is not of a particularly
involved kind, and, indeed, there are a number of simple and compound sentences. In McEwan's first three novels, linguistic sophistication is marked and surely serves as a self-referential device,
focusing the reader's attention on the text and the act of narration
(and thus raising questions about the partiality of any account). As
in *The Innocent*, this element seems much less marked in *Black
Dogs*. Where it does occur, it seems primarily motivated by Jeremy's
character and upbringing. He writes of his manner of speech as an
adolescent, "the rather formal, distancing, labyrinthine tone in
which I used to speak . . . which was supposed to announce me to
the world as an intellectual" (xviii), and one may assume that some
habits remain. For example, his observations about scorpions bear
the mark of a kind of adolescent pedantry (93–94). Here, however,
such passages fulfill a different function in the text from that in

McEwan's first three novels. They enhance the verisimilitude of the novel ("Ah yes, Jeremy would speak just like that . . . ," the reader says), rather than call attention to the text itself and its linguistic substance.

In terms of genre, too, *Black Dogs* also shows a shift in comparison to McEwan's earlier novels, a shift from self-referentiality toward a kind of transparency and self-effacement. While it is, in many ways, no less literary a text than its predecessors, it achieves that foregrounded textuality through different, but related, methods. Certainly, there are elements of genre mixture in *Black Dogs*, but they are not as marked as in McEwan's earlier fiction. The text has in part the status of a "memoir," both of the Tremaines and Jeremy himself. It is an account of the Tremaines' life, especially of the events of 1946 that are so crucial for their marriage, and of Jeremy's own adolescence and his fascination with the diametrically opposed views of his parents-in-law. The text starts off with Jeremy's recollection of his own past, and, to some extent, the whole novel becomes an act of self-scrutiny, and thus a psychological study of the Tremaines and of their son-in-law (see pages xxi-xxii, for example).

The question of belief, so prominently raised by the narrator throughout the novel, is of crucial importance in the text. At one point Jeremy describes his parents-in-law thus: "Rationalist and mystic, commissar and yogi, joiner and abstainer, scientist and intuitionist, Bernard and June are the extremities, the twin poles along whose slippery axis my own unbelief slithers and never comes to rest" (xxiii). The echo of Arthur Koestler's celebrated essay of 1945, "The Yogi and the Commissar," suggests how *Black Dogs* has a discursive, essaylike element in it.[4] The two positions—that of June (belief in some kind of deity, in some kind of intermittently benign order in the universe, in the spirit) and that of Bernard (an insistence on the importance of rationalism, on the absence of a controlling deity, on a material understanding of the world)—are set out in the novel, as if they were two possible views of the universe being discussed in an essay. At one point, for example, in the passage concerning the aftermath of Jeremy's encounter with a scorpion, the text becomes clearly dialogue-like, with the voices of June and Bernard giving different interpretations of the incident (94–97). The text is both a psychological study and, to some extent, a philosophical novel, in which different intellectual and moral positions are constantly in dialogue with each other. Thus genre mixture, and its accompanying reminder of textuality, is present in *Black Dogs,* although not to the same degree as in other earlier texts by McEwan.

If narration, language, and genre do not appear to have any self-referential function in *Black Dogs,* the same cannot be said of narrative (that is, the ordering of events within the text). This narrative foregrounds and underlines the process of telling stories and giving accounts by its frequent shifts from one setting to another. In Parts One and Two of the novel these occur very frequently. Jeremy describes his "memoir" as really a "divagation" (a wandering, a set of digressions) (15), and also notes at one point a tendency "to leapfrog" over periods of time (18). Indeed, this is how his narrative proceeds. On page 16 the reader leaps from the mid-1980s to France in 1938; on page 18 from 1938 back to 1987 and then to 1946; on page 20 the reader returns to the novel's present again. Page 23 marks a shift from the 1980s to 1944, and after returning to 1987 the narrative leaps back to the 1940s again toward the end of part 1 (38). Bernard and Jeremy's journey to Berlin in 1989 is marked by constant shifts between the present and the 1940s (53, 54, 56, 57). In part 3 the sight of an airport destination board in Berlin in 1989 makes Jeremy recall incidents in Poland in 1981 (83). When those have been told, he returns to the late 1980s again (90). The act of telling the stories that make up *Black Dogs* is thus emphasized. One can never ignore the text itself as it constantly oscillates between different time periods. And this act of telling is further emphasized in the novel's final part 4, which, in recounting the crucial moment of the meeting with the black dogs, goes back over information that the reader already has (111, 115, 116). The reader is never in this novel allowed to forget that he/she is being told a story.[5]

Other features also draw sharp attention to the novel as artifact and text. First, there are frequent overt literary allusions in the text, reminding the reader of the literary nature of the material before him/her. For example, Proust is referred to on two occasions (xv, xix). Kafka, too, is mentioned (xix). "Love, to borrow Sylvia Plath's phrase, set me going," the narrator remarks (xxi). Jeremy brings Boswell's journal to June when he comes to write down, like Boswell for Dr. Johnson, her words (10). When Jeremy writes of visiting Majdanek, he echoes Conrad's *Heart of Darkness* by referring to "the dreamers of the nightmare" (88).[6] Although not strictly literary, but rather historical, Jeremy's vision of himself as a figure from French history, when he challenges the violent father in the hotel, also has marked literary overtones (107). It may be argued that these allusions are simply appropriate to Jeremy's literary interests and thus no more than character-building devices (and they certainly are that). But they also give a distinctly literary flavor to the whole text, perhaps also reminding one of its literary and its made nature.

The second way in which the text foregrounds its textuality, its status as a story, is by simply being such an obviously carefully assembled piece of craftsmanship on the part of the implied author. For example, the incident in the hotel in part 3—in which Jeremy comes to the rescue of an abused small French boy—cleverly dovetails with the novel's central motifs: the family, the fractured family, violence, the dogs (Jeremy is stopped from seriously injuring the boy's father by a French lady's peremptory "Ça suffit" (That's enough) (101, 108), something one says to misbehaving dogs). It even echoes minor motifs, like the kicks which form part of the attack on Bernard in Berlin and which here are about to be meted out to the fallen Frenchman by Jeremy (75, 108). The same may be said of the neo-Fascist skinheads in Berlin and the black dogs themselves. Both obviously echo each other, masterless, "loose, wet mouths," "heads and tongues lolling" (73–74, 122–23). The hand of the implied author is very evident at times.

Third, the novel advertises its own technique through a constant and teasing building of suspense. This is noted by Bette Pesetsky in her review in *The New York Times Book Review*.[7] The reader learns of the black dogs and of the incident in 1946 early in the text, and thereafter there are numerous references to the importance of that day, to its consequences for June and Bernard, to its metaphorical significance, and to details of the event ("What those dogs had been trained to do?" [*sic*] [82]), but without the incident as a whole being fully presented (xxii–xxiii, 6, 18, 20, 26, 82–83). It is only in the final chapter that the reader learns in detail about the incident of the dogs. The very reversal of chronology itself reminds one of the implied author and the particularity of this telling of the events.

Fourth, in common with some of McEwan's other novels, *Black Dogs* is a novel of fragments (carefully integrated, but still clearly fragments). This is most marked in the Berlin section (part 2), the reminiscence of the visit to Poland in 1981 (83–90), the incident of the scorpion (90–98), the section dealing with Jeremy's fight in the hotel (101–8), and in the final black dogs chapter itself (part 4). Each of these is a separate narrative with a clearly defined beginning and end and with an appropriate pattern of conflict and climax. All have some kind of resolution, too. It is this building up of a novel out of self-contained shorter narratives which works, as genre mixture does in other novels, to draw attention to the textuality, the madeness of the novel as a whole. As genre mixture shocks the reader into a special kind of awareness by its transitions, so the fragmentariness of the text serves to highlight textuality. Once again, McEwan's fiction shows an interesting shift of technique over the course of several novels. This fragmentariness can be observed in *The Child in Time* (the kidnapping in the supermarket [11–19] and the incident in which Stephen climbs Charles's beech tree [122–32]) and in *The Innocent* (the account of Oscar's dismemberment [ch. 18]), in which certain episodes seem to isolate themselves from the rest of the text as discrete mininarratives, almost as separate short stories set apart from the remainder of the novel. But this is even more marked in *Black Dogs* because there are more of these fragment narratives, and also because the novel itself is shorter than its two predecessors.[8]

At this point it will be useful to sum up what has been observed with regard to narration, language, genre, narrative, and literary allusion. What is this complex interplay of elements all for? The answer is relatively simple. All these elements have several functions in the text (and some of these will be noted later), but they combine to give the novel a particular tension. *Black Dogs* vacillates, as does much of McEwan's later fiction, between a conservatism, a traditionality of technique which aims at transparency of the text and lack of any kind of problematization, on one hand, and a technique which foregrounds text and draws attention to the textual nature of what is before the reader, on the other. This interweaving of contradictory elements creates an interesting dynamism in the text and is also very appropriate to another major aspect of the novel—its emphasis on the problems of knowing the truth and of storytelling, and its resolution of those problems—which will be discussed below.

For *Black Dogs*, like *The Innocent*, is about a brush (or two) with history, and how one makes sense of that in narrative account. As with so many contemporary novels, *Black Dogs* is steeped in the events and processes of history. The text abounds in dates: 1946 (3), 1956 (5), 1983 (8), "five years on" (8), 1987 (8), 1938 (16), "the early months of 1944" (23), "a little more than two years later" (45), "October 1981" (83), "in the spring of 1946" (111), "I'm talking of '40 and '41" (132), "April 1944" (135). The quasi epilogue in part 4 gives details of June's and Bernard's lives after 1946, and it does so through a precisely dated chronology (145–47). Events have to be labeled with dates, marked out in time, as if the novel were a history and it were necessary to locate those events along a chronology.

References to major historical events and processes are also frequent, and these are closely related to the actions or fates of the novel's characters. Bernard stays in the Communist Party "until the Soviet invasion of Hungary in 1956" (5). He phones Jeremy in tremendous excitement as he watches the Berlin Wall collapse in 1989. He, and later Jeremy too, feels an impulse to see historic events take place at first hand. "History was happening," Jeremy reflects, "without me" (47–48). A complete section (part 2) is taken up with the sights and sounds of Berlin in that historic November of

BRUSHES WITH HISTORY (II)

1989. At one point the narrator and his father-in-law stand in the historically loaded setting of the Reichstag building and Gestapo headquarters (now being excavated and investigated by archaeologists) (70). And the events of the evening are visited by more active reminders of Germany's past. The skinheads who attack Bernard sport swastika tattoos and shout "Ausländer 'raus!" (Foreigners out!), echoing their spiritual forebears in the 1930s (73, 82). Jeremy's visit to Poland coincides with the tension and dynamism of Solidarity's activities just before General Jaruzelski's introduction of martial law in 1981 (83–90). "There was only one conversation. Poland. Its urgency swirled around us and pressed in as we moved from one dim, grubby room, one cigarette haze to another" (84). Jeremy and Jenny fall in love against this background of international events and against that of the Majdanek concentration camp (90). June and Bernard travel through a Europe devastated by World War II (113). The Maire's story is of events driven by that war: resistance, German repression, betrayal, and brutality (132–36). The black dogs themselves surely cry out to be interpreted as metaphors of a brutal and recurrent history. A legacy of particular historical events, the dogs, in June's vision, "will return to haunt us, somewhere in Europe, in another time" (149).[9]

In addition, the narrator of *Black Dogs* is a man fascinated by the past, its difference from the present, and yet the present's rootedness in that past. This fascination is marked by the frequent movements of the narrative into the past. *Black Dogs* (as noted earlier) obsessively shifts from present to past. Above all, Jeremy is fascinated with the past and its difference from, yet relationship with, the present. The novel proper starts with him considering and reflecting on a snapshot of his parents-in-law in 1946, taken just before their

journey to Italy and France. He notes details of their appearance and
speculates about the circumstances surrounding the photograph. He
is clearly fascinated (in fact, he uses the word "fascination" on page
4) by June and Bernard's past. Bernard has stayed essentially
unchanged, he notes, in the forty or more years since the photograph
was taken; June, however, has changed almost beyond recognition.
The detail in which he describes her young self shows an interest in
the sheer pastness of a distant time, its substantial differences in
clothing, artifacts, moral-social attitudes, and modes of behavior (4).
Jeremy's interest in his parents-in-law is, however, not just a matter
of dress. Their political concerns—they have just joined the Communist Party and are full of optimism about the future of the world
and the benign changes that they are sure will soon come with cap-
italism's demise—are also set out (4–5). These early passages are
representative of many others in the novel. Jeremy pursues his parents-in-law into their pasts, lovingly recording details of dress and
mentality, noting differences between past and present yet also trying to understand how the present grew out of that particular past.

A few pages later, he returns to the photograph and reflects on
the strange "innocence" of faces in the photograph, an innocence
which he sees as coming from a seeming unawareness of the future
passage of time and its changes (14). Looking from June to the photograph, Jeremy formulates for himself the whole motive of his
memoir gathering. "The question I really wanted to ask was, How
did you get from that face to this, how did you end up looking so
extraordinary—was it the life? My, how you've changed!" (15). In
the course of their conversations, June confronts Jeremy with his
inability to understand the past. She tries to explain her sexual
obsession with Bernard to a man from another generation who can

barely imagine sexual passion in such a different world (31). But over the next few pages June attempts to correct Jeremy's notion of the past, setting out the young lovers' passion and a context of disapproval and danger. She also places their political concerns, their political passions, in the circumstances of their physical and emotional obsession with each other (32–35). A fascination with the past is also represented by the narrator's interest in the incident of the black dogs. He and his wife, as well as Bernard and June, return to it constantly throughout the novel. Finally, in part 4 one is given the full details of the incident which has radically altered two people's marriage and deeply influenced their children. As is so common in British novels of McEwan's generation of writers, the past—history—is everywhere, a point of fascination, sheerly different, but an inescapable influence on the present.

Yet, as is also so common in contemporary British fiction, *Black Dogs* makes problematic the very possibility of giving an account of the past that is the object of fascinated examination. It does this by the self-referential aspects of narrative and literary allusion discussed above. But the novel also employs a number of other means to do so—by reminding the reader of the mode of transmission of the material in the novel itself, by emphasizing the unreliability of memory and the partiality of any version of events, and by foregrounding motifs of interpretation.

Readers are reminded on a few occasions of how they come to be in possession of Jeremy's narrative. It is announced as a "memoir" and as one in which "a number of liberties" have been taken, "the most flagrant of which has been to recount certain conversations never intended for the record" (xxiv). Readers are reminded that the text is a text, and one subject to manipulation. They are also reminded that everything has been written in shorthand and then decoded into roman letters, thus emphasizing the process of textual making and transmission (10, 147). But above all, the fallibility of memory and the unreliability of any version of events are stressed. Jeremy reflects that his memory of the weather during his last visits to June in 1987 may be wrong (6). When June settles back to recall the traumatic events of 1946, Jeremy reflects, "Each time it came out a little differently" (16). Jeremy's memory of the Polish countryside is "unreliable" (87).

Closely connected with the unreliability of memory in this novel is its stress on the partiality, the limited accuracy, of any account. The narrator questions the trustworthiness of June's memory and suspects that he is being used to transmit a particular version ("the final fix") of the events of his mother-in-law's life (17). He certainly knows that the account she gives of her husband's present circumstances is a parody of the truth (20–21). Bernard and June give quite different versions of their first meetings (23–25), and Jeremy at times sees the "turning point" of the black dogs incident as too convenient, too neat, too literary an explanation of June's life (27). The couple's early lovemaking and the incident in which Bernard stands Tarzan-like at an open window are presented quite differently by the two participants (34, 63). Bernard even claims that June gets facts and setting wrong (63). "What was she doing, making that up?" he exclaims. "Cooking the books, that's what! . . . She's rewritten it for the official version. It's the airbrush all over again" (63). Immediately afterward, he attacks June again for falsifying accounts of events (63–64).

The issue here is not whether Bernard is right, but rather that accounts may well be unreliable. Bernard himself knows how easy it is to lie about events. He knows it from his ten years in the Communist Party ("If you ignored or reshaped a few uncomfortable facts for the cause of Party unity . . ." [66]) and (paradoxically, it might seem) from his work as a scientist ("Laboratory work teaches you better than anything how easy it is to bend a result to fit a theory . . ." [66–67]). Late in the novel, Madame Auriac retells June's story of the dogs "with only minor embellishments" (but with those embellishments) (130), while she and the Maire disagree about the "simple truth" of the outcast Danielle (136).

Black Dogs, however, is not simply full of partial accounts of facts, but also emphasizes the process of the interpretation of any facts and how different interpretations may be. On one occasion, this is quite comic. The novel starts with a sentence that is ambiguous and open to differing interpretations. "Ever since I lost mine in a road accident when I was eight, I have had my eye on other people's parents" (xiii). What did Jeremy lose: his eye or his parents? The reader works out the correct answer very quickly, but for a moment, at least, the sentence is open to two interpretations. How one looks at photographs, also, Jeremy argues, depends on where one is. "Fifty years on" one may look as strange or as naive in them as do one's forebears (15). Above all, the central events of the novel are made open to Bernard's rationalistic interpretation or to June's metaphysical one (xxii-xxiii). For June the encounter with the dogs is an encounter with absolute evil and with a saving Godlike principle (37). For Bernard this is "religious cant," the dogs themselves a literary borrowing (from Churchill, from Dr. Johnson), and the whole business interpreted so as to allow June to take a path she had already decided upon (82). In the aftermath of the incident with the scorpion, Jeremy hears in his head June and Bernard giving their differing interpretations of the occurrence (94–97). Toward the end of the novel, the reader is again confronted with sentences that require interpretation. All the sentences that suggest that Danielle has been raped not by the Gestapo but by their dog are incomplete (135–36). The reader is required to supply the ending based on an interpretation of context. One of the key revelations of the text turns out to be based not just on fallible account (which it is), but on the reader's own process of interpretation.

However, June and Bernard's story *can* be told. Despite the doubts that the novel casts on the possibility of any accurate narrative account of past events, it ends with just such an authoritative and authorized presentation of what happened that day in June 1946 in Southern France. Unashamedly using the traditional technique of a third-person omniscient narrator (moving between June's and Bernard's point of view), with all the detailed description of landscape and evocation of social and historical background, all the psychological detail of a traditional prose narrative, Jeremy gives us what is being presented as the truth. There are three ways to interpret this. First, McEwan may be simply being incompetent here (and that is the view of Coster in the *London Review of Books*).[10] This is unlikely. McEwan by the time he publishes his fifth novel has demonstrated that he is a competent professional writer. The second way to interpret the novel's conclusion is that finally this is only one specific narrator's version of events, and is as much to be called into question as June's or Bernard's account of their first meeting and lovemaking. The third way, however, is to suggest that this conclusion to the novel implies that, despite all the difficulties connected with telling history, recounting events is possible in a credible and useful way. The story *can*, after all, be told in a way that seems ultimately acceptable. This last way of reading the ending dovetails with the dynamic tension in *Black Dogs* noted above. Texts give access to events, and those texts are partial and limited. But that is not all one can say about the relation of narrative to events. Certain traditional, unproblematized ways of telling (a verisimilar narrational technique, referential rather than self-referential language, lack of radical genre shifts) have a power and authority that are not wholly to be despised. The story *can* be told with some probable accuracy and authority.

The novel's opening sentence and the passages concerning Danielle's rape are, finally, rather unusual in *Black Dogs*. Here the novel's thematic concerns (about the reliability of narratives) are transferred onto a technical level; elsewhere they seem to exist only on a thematic one. This means that they are present as a subject matter or topic, rather than as part of how the novel is made. In McEwan's earlier fiction, up to *The Innocent* although most markedly in his first three novels, concerns about reliability of account and metafictional matters permeate many aspects of the text, from narration and language to generic elements. *Black Dogs*, however, seems to present the paradox of a text that is technically rather unproblematic but that raises numerous issues concerning the problematic nature of texts, and that finally suggests one can tell a story with some degree of accuracy. Whether this is a significant development in McEwan's own fiction, or in British fiction at large, is a question that requires time and further analysis for its answer.

The question of the partiality of any account of things is embodied in the dispute that is the central focus of *Black Dogs*. June and Bernard just simply see the world (or come to see the world) in radically different ways. The novel is, in part, a weighing up, as far as fiction can do so, of two of the central themes of Western civilization: the claims of metaphysical, religious belief and materialist rationality.

The novel is to some extent organized as a debate between June and Bernard, with Jeremy as an undecided observer ripe for conversion ("I had no attachments. I believed in nothing" [xxii]). One critic, at least, has found the characters in *Black Dogs* too schematic, and certainly they can seem that way: Jeremy all uncertainty; Bernard all bluff commonsense rationalism; June all private mysticism.[11] The novel is organized around a clash of the rational and the nonrational, of practical political activity and private mysticism. Jeremy—almost too neatly—sums up this clash and its embodiment in the novel's protagonists. "Rationalist and mystic, commissar and yogi, joiner and abstainer, scientist and intuitionist, Bernard and June are the extremities, the twin poles along which my own unbelief slithers and never comes to rest"(xxiii). June insists that a concern with this world, with politics, and with social activity leads to an impoverishment, a lack of appreciation for the richness and beauty of that very world and the mysterious divine force that underlies it (19–20). There is a mysterious "power of love" in the universe that Bernard and his kind simply ignore (36–37). Bernard talks of practical political matters (will Germany be reunified or not?) and does so through methodical, logical argument (50–51). He finds June's mind driven by rather absurd emotions (for example, outrage at killing an insect in the cause of science) (55–57), and he is extremely vexed by what he sees as her lack of respect for any kind of objective, verifiable truth (63–64). They come together as voices in Jeremy's head as he considers the incident with the scorpion in part 3. June's voice advances nonrational explanations for his not touching the switchboard cupboard and, thus, not being bitten by a scorpion; Bernard's dismisses these and gives his own rational, materialistic ones (94–97).

This dispute between the two relates to an opposition that runs throughout McEwan's fiction, an opposition between male and female. It takes varying forms in *The Cement Garden*, *The Comfort of Strangers*, *The Child in Time*, and *The Innocent*, and in *Black Dogs* it is evident that the clash of intuition and reason is related to the genders of the principal characters. At one point Jeremy talks of clearing his throat as "a sceptical, masculine sound" (91), while earlier, Bernard has seen one of his arguments with June as illustrating the differences between men's (rational) and women's (magical) ways of thinking (57). One should, nonetheless, note that Jeremy (a man) himself is undecided in the whole matter of the rational or the nonrational, while his wife, Jenny, is clearly "sensible, efficient" and highly successful in the world (57). Certainly, the dispute between the two characters remains unresolved at the novel's end. What were the black dogs—fiends from the pit, subject to some rational explanation (German military dogs run wild), June's own self-delusive myth? One does not know, and perhaps McEwan wishes to suggest that the quarrel between Bernard's and June's positions cannot be resolved in any final way.

There are two other major groups of motifs in *Black Dogs* that seem related in some way to June and Bernard's dispute. It has already been noted how characters' lives and experiences are closely related to public and historical events. For example, Jeremy and Jenny's lovemaking is interrupted by Bernard's excited telephone call about the fall of the Berlin Wall (46–47). But one of the clearest ways in which private and public are interwoven is embodied in

another major strand of motifs that runs throughout *Black Dogs*. The
novel continually presents violence and a rejection of civilization.
Violence is clearly there in Jeremy's youth, in the sadistic-masochis-
tic relationship of his sister and her husband, in their treatment of
each other and of their daughter (xx). The whole episode connected
with Jeremy and Bernard's visit to the Berlin Wall bubbles with violence (72–76). The unimaginable violence of Majdanek (87–89), the
French father's brutal violence toward his child (106) and Jeremy's
response (108), the hideous black dogs themselves (126)—all embody
a brutal savagery that, Jeremy suggests, will recur in Europe sometime in the future (149). Even Bernard's killing of an insect
becomes, for June, representative of a monstrous human cruelty
(55–56). As is often the case in McEwan's fiction, the child is an
important focus in *Black Dogs*: here as a victim of brutality.
Jeremy's niece Sally and the boy in the French restaurant both
embody this. It is also worth noting that June is pregnant with her
first child when she is attacked by the dogs.

Violence is closely connected with an abandonment of civilization. This is how Jeremy sees his friends at the novel's start: as
young men who are turning from their parents' intellectual culture
toward something more brutal and racy (xv-xviii). The skinheads
who attack Bernard have cut themselves loose from decency and
humanity. They have become animal-like in appearance and behavior (73–74). Majdanek is the antithesis of the city and the life near
which it stood (87). The black dogs, June feels, reverse the common
expectations of our culture and civilization by attacking her
(122–23). Sometime in the future, she believes, they will come back
and convulse Europe again (147). Of course, in the novel things are
not quite as simple as that. When June and Bernard begin their love

affair, they reject the norms of their time and place; they turn from that civilization, and, the novel suggests, are right to do so (33–35). Majdanek is orderly and well made (features often connected with good civilizations), yet is also monstrous (88–89). Bernard is saved from a beating by the wild, street ferocity of the young woman in Berlin, not by the power of sensible argument (75–76). Jeremy resorts to fairly savage violence to express his disapproval of the French father's striking his child (108).

How does all this connect: the novel's contrast of the rational and the nonrational with its presentation of violence and a rejection of civilization? Perhaps it does not do so as clearly as one might hope. As is the case with *The Child in Time*, one has an uneasy sense that the novel as a whole might not cohere, however fascinating and brilliant it might be in its separate parts. But perhaps the novel does achieve a kind of coherence by suggesting that both rationality and nonrationality can lead to violence and the breakdown of civilized norms. The parents who torment their children are driven by, surely, nonrational forces; Majdanek and Communism's crimes in the name of humanity are monuments to perverted rationality. And, on the other hand, one sometimes must have recourse to the nonrational—the young woman in Berlin who saves Bernard, Jeremy in the French restaurant (though it is difficult to see what he achieves by beating up the boy's father), and, of course, June's fighting off the black dogs. Perhaps the point is that neither rationality nor nonrationality is completely right or solves the problem. The problem is that the black dogs will return, mysterious metaphors of individual human wickedness and of European madness, or horridly rational products of that madness.

The novel suggests that only love redeems the situation. Bernard and June's relationship has been both a failure and a success. They could not live together, but they did stay together. If both have a sense of failure, it is because they could not realize or make tangible that love. But Jeremy's life does give some cause for hope. His marriage is a good one; his children are loved. That is no mean achievement in the world of the novel (even if, in literary and moral terms, it is a very Victorian solution to the world's problems).

"But it is the black dogs I return to most often," Jeremy declares at the end of the novel. They run off not as real animals, but as "incarnations," into a desolate landscape that is part Southern France, part dream, and from there "they will return to haunt us, somewhere in Europe, in another time" (148–49). The novel ends on a dark note. Neither the rationalist nor the mystic will save us, nor will love. The somber conclusion of this ambitious novel, with its powerful metaphor of the black dogs, haunts one's mind long after one has finished reading.

CHAPTER EIGHT

Science and Fictions
Enduring Love

Bernard in *Black Dogs* is a rationalist and amateur scientist; Thelma in *The Child in Time* is a scientist, teacher of science, and expounder of scientific ideas; June in *Black Dogs* is a mystic with strong, if not wholly defined, religious feelings. All three are also lovers in their own ways. Similar characters—the scientific rationalist, the lover, the mystic—come together again to shape the central focus of McEwan's sixth novel, *Enduring Love* (1997). Joe is a writer on science, popularizer of scientific theories, and tireless advocate of rationalism and materialism. He loves deeply the beautiful Clarissa, with whom he has lived in an informal marriage for several years. Much of the novel's action is motivated by someone's falling in love with him: the obsessive, religious Jed. The clash of world views observed in *Black Dogs* and its interweaving with love between two characters drive a very serious and powerful novel.

Enduring Love looks again at several concerns that run throughout McEwan's fiction. Like *The Cement Garden*, *The Comfort of Strangers*, *The Child in Time*, and *The Innocent*, it is a study of extreme and, in part, deeply disturbed psychological states. Jed's obsession and Joe's desperate clinging to his sanity in the face of his stalker are echoes of pathological states—incestuous longings (Jack in *The Cement Garden*), sadistic erotic practices (Robert and Caroline in *The Comfort of Strangers*), and deep psychological trauma (Stephen in *The Child in Time*, Maria and Leonard in *The Innocent*)

—in the earlier novels. The way in which it is so easy to step from stability and normality into horror that is so pronounced an aspect of *Enduring Love* is part, too, of the earlier novels. In *Enduring Love*, Joe is one minute a happy, successful man with a beautiful lover; the next minute, he is plunged into a nightmare of another's obsession with him. Similarly, in *The Comfort of Strangers* Colin and Mary turn the wrong corner in a foreign city and find the murderous Robert waiting for them. Stephen in *The Child in Time* simply goes shopping on a Saturday morning with his daughter and loses everything in a matter of moments: child, wife, happiness. On the night of their engagement party the happy lovers, Maria and Leonard, move from love and joy to brutal butchery (*The Innocent*). June walks a few hundred yards ahead of Bernard on their hike through the French countryside and suddenly finds herself fighting for her life and living through an experience that will undermine her marriage. Open the wrong door, turn down the wrong street, lose attention for a moment, McEwan suggests, and you can step into a nightmare. And—as the examples just given might indicate— although McEwan is often seen as a writer who argues for the redeeming power of human love, he is also one who suggests love's fragility. Colin and Mary step toward their destruction half-knowingly (*The Comfort of Strangers*); Stephen and Julia's marriage breaks down under, admittedly, terrible pressure (*The Child in Time*); Maria and Leonard's love cannot survive crime and separation (*The Innocent*); Bernard and June are unable to live together after the encounter with the dogs (*Black Dogs*). Similarly, *Enduring Love* depicts in some detail how Jed's advances drive Joe and Clarissa apart. Love seems a fragile thing here and elsewhere in McEwan's fiction.

SCIENCE AND FICTIONS

Questions of knowledge—epistemological questions, how much one can know, how one can know anything—are frequent in McEwan's novels. The way in which Colin and Mary scarcely ever share the same viewpoint, and the manner in which the novel draws attention to its own textual substance in *The Comfort of Strangers*; the fascination with relativity, fictions, and illusions in *The Child in Time* and *The Innocent*; the clash of two radically different views of the world in *Black Dogs*—all these form an important aspect of McEwan's fiction. This concern with the difficulties of knowing and understanding the world is very prominent in *Enduring Love*, which takes the form of a kind of epistemological thriller. In *Enduring Love* Joe is a rationalist and proponent of scientific knowledge and method, and his interest in science is clearly very relevant to McEwan's overall fascination with problems of knowledge. References to science are very prominent in *The Child in Time* and in *Black Dogs*, and they also run through McEwan's oratorio *Or Shall We Die?* and his television screenplay *The Imitation Game*.[1]

However, *Enduring Love* is not simply a reprise of old material, but a probing in a fresh context of certain concerns that permeate McEwan's output. This probing takes the form of a powerful and ultimately quite ambitious novel. It is a love story of sorts. After a suspenseful opening in which a secondary character dies in a ballooning accident, the novel shows how the protagonist Joe (a successful writer on scientific subjects, in a long-term relationship with the beautiful Clarissa) finds that he has become the object of the obsessive homosexual affections of a chance-met stranger, the unstable and religious Jed. (McEwan never uses the term "stalk" in the novel, but this is what Jed does to Joe.) Joe works out that Jed suffers from a psychological disturbance called de Clérambault's syndrome.[2] He also discovers that no one around him accepts his diagnosis. De Clérambault's syndrome is a type of erotomania that involves the obsessional love of another person, often of higher social status. The lover is convinced that the loved one reciprocates his or her love but cannot show it directly. The lover is further convinced that the loved one is really sending him or her secret messages of encouragement, incomprehensible to others, even though the loved one denies doing so. This is truly a type of enduring love, in that it is immune to denial and disproof and may, indeed, last forever. It can also turn into hatred and violence, as it does in *Enduring Love*.

The reception of *Enduring Love* is the usual mixed one that greets McEwan's recent fiction. There are some very positive voices. For example, Merritt Moseley in the *Sewanee Review* notes that "I read *Enduring Love* when it first came out and thought it must be the best British novel of 1997," although he adds that when he read John Banville's *The Untouchable* (which is not, of course, a British novel), he thought Banville's novel better. In the *Spectator*, Anita Brookner (and surely the esteem of this very eminent novelist counts for a lot) praises *Enduring Love* highly, writing of "Ian McEwan's clever, even brilliant novel" and insisting that "McEwan has contrived a marvelous fiction on the basis of fact . . . , yet it remains an imaginative reconstruction of a superior kind." However, in the *New Statesman*, Amanda Craig, while admiring the novel's suspense and its excellence as a "psychological thriller," bemoans its rehashing of well-known scientific ideas, its "schematic" opposition between Joe and Jed, and a "silliness" (unspecified) that the critic finds in McEwan's "fascination with the scientific and the supernatural." It is a schematic element in the novel's central opposition that irks Adam Mars-Jones in the *Observer,* too. He suggests that the novel shows "an inability fully to dramatize its themes" and finds it "disappointing that a book that begins so full-throatedly should end with stagy confrontation." And in a rather disenchanted overview of McEwan's fiction in *Prospect* in late 1998, Jason Cowley argues that *Enduring Love* "is caged, like all his [McEwan's] later work, within an over-determined, intensely schematic structure." However, there are other, positive verdicts, such as Donna Seaman's in *Booklist*, where the critic writes that "McEwan, a master stylist, has the complex psychology of this extreme yet credible situation [Jed's stalking Joe] down pat, managing, too, to subtly transform the struggle between Joe and Jed into a life-or-death battle between reason and faith, rationality and madness."[3]

Enduring Love is a traditional and accessible novel without any substantial degree of experimentation in terms of narrative and narration. Events are recounted in a logical-chronological, linear fashion, and where there are retrospects, these are clearly marked (for example, in chapter 12).[4] The story material has all the exciting elements and suspense of a thriller. Will the boy in the balloon be saved? Will Joe persuade the rest of the world that Jed is harassing him? Will Jed's hired killers succeed in murdering him? Will Joe save Clarissa? Cliffhangers and climaxes abound, and the novel builds up to a very traditional climactic confrontation between Joe and Jed. The appendix to the novel even performs the function of an epilogue or concluding chapter in a Victorian novel by satisfying the reader's curiosity about what happens after the main action ends.

The novel is largely narrated from a traditional first-person perspective. Joe recounts almost the entire story, although on five occasions other narrators have their say. Chapter 23 takes the form of a brief letter from Clarissa to Joe, in which she gives her version of some of the events she has observed. Her point of view is given in one other place, in chapter 9. However, it is important to note that she does not speak for herself in this second chapter, but rather that Joe adopts her point of view and narrates the circumstances of a bitter quarrel between the two of them through her thoughts and feelings. (The implications of Joe's doing this are important and will be considered later.) Jed speaks directly to the reader on three occasions, each time through letters (chs. 11, 16, and appendix 2). These are largely rhapsodic effusions of love for Joe, but they also have narrative elements, especially the first two letters. But in all three cases, Jed is scarcely allowed to speak for himself. Joe (or the implied author of the novel—this is not clear from the text) has selected the two letters in the body of the novel from dozens that are sent to him. The third is taken from Jed's patient's notes at the psychiatric hospital where he is confined, and is also one of hundreds (for he writes every day) he has written to his beloved Joe. Like Kurtz in Conrad's *Heart of Darkness* or Heathcliff in Emily Brontë's *Wuthering Heights*, the disruptive, dangerous Jed is rarely allowed to speak directly to the reader, and then only through the filter of another's control.

Narration is, thus, deeply traditional in *Enduring Love*, as it is in most of McEwan's fiction apart from *The Cement Garden*. A substantially reliable first-person narrator gives an account of events. The utterances of other characters are largely contained within this character's narration and are under his control. The only point where Joe might be said to relinquish control of the narration is in appendix 1, which takes the form of an article supposedly reprinted from the *British Review of Psychiatry*, written by two psychiatrists about Jed's case. This is a pastiche of a scientific paper, with the appropriate layout, narrative organization, conclusions, and references. But, in a sense, Joe's perspective has not been abandoned. Like him, the authors of the paper are men of science, and everything they write reinforces what Joe has been saying throughout the novel. Jed is dangerous, does show the symptoms of de Clérambault's syndrome, and should be locked up. Almost everything in the novel goes to provide a unified point of view on the action, a point of view that is reliable and authenticated by such other perspectives as the novel gives. The reader is surely meant to feel at ease about Joe's account, and to believe and trust him. (Just as one is meant to trust Jeremy in *Black Dogs*, although not Jack in *The Cement Garden*.)

The action of *Enduring Love* is open, as is the case with many of McEwan's novels, to the charge of fragmentariness. In his essay on McEwan's fiction, Cowley notes that "most" of McEwan's novels, "including *Enduring Love*," are "narratives of moments: a series of imaginative set pieces which seldom coagulate into a fully realized work."[5] If this argument is true (and it is at least moot), then the opening two chapters of *Enduring Love*, which give a knuckle-clenching account of a fatal ballooning accident, would be prime examples of this seeming fragmentariness. As in some of McEwan's other novels, certain episodes seem to stand out as complete in themselves and somehow separate from the novel's main story material. Although they are set within it, they also seem distinct fragments which could conceivably stand on their own as mininarratives. In *Enduring Love* this is also true of chapter 21, in which Joe buys a gun. This fragmentariness is something that runs throughout McEwan's fiction and something that has been mentioned in previous chapters.

Enduring Love shows signs of the thriller or crime story. Joe is stalked by a dangerous young man who eventually makes an attempt on his life. The novel's climax involves Jed's holding Clarissa at knifepoint and Joe's shooting Jed in the arm. But, despite this, the dominant focus of the novel is on characters' psychology. In its way it is a version of a very traditional, triangular, psychological love story, a version of the kind of fiction that explores characters' minds and feelings in respect of each other. Appendix 1, the article from the *British Review of Psychiatry*, is a clear indication of the novel's psychological interests.[6] The novel itself takes the form of an intricate analysis of the three central characters' states of mind.

One sees least of Clarissa but is told quite a lot about her, although it must be remembered that the source of one's knowledge is Joe (even in chapter 9 when her point of view is ostentatiously adopted). The reader knows that she is unable to have children, and Joe indicates that this is a key aspect of her life. She is devoted to several godchildren (34–35), and Joe even sees the lack of children in their relationship as underlying a discussion of a relatively unconnected topic (75). Her motive for choosing Joe as her partner is suggested: her father has suffered from Alzheimer's disease; she wants the security of the extremely rational Joe (90). But she herself is someone driven by emotions rather than by logic and reason, and at times she finds Joe's steady rationality absurd and unnerving (36, 159). It is important in this respect that she is involved with the humanities rather than the sciences and is an expert on Keats's love poetry and letters rather than, for example, theoretical physics. Chapter 9 is an attempt by Joe to capture the complex ebb and flow of her feelings as she comes home to a disturbed and overexcited partner, and the complexity of her feelings is well represented when she blames Joe himself for the whole unfortunate mess (110) and, once she has decided to leave him, becomes excited at the prospect of a new life (161). Clarissa is allowed to speak for herself in chapter 23, and here one is given a rather different view of the events of the novel. She sees Joe as having overreacted to Jed's advances, as having isolated himself from her, and even as having found in Jed a way out of his own guilt with regard to the ballooning accident. Clarissa is a complicated figure in her own right, seen in some depth, who adds a degree of psychological complexity to the picture of the two main characters.

Jed is literally a psychological case study. His highly disturbed emotional state is analyzed in the language of psychiatry in appendix 1, and his erotomania (devoted love turning into violence) and what it leads to form one of the novel's central focuses. The psychiatric article even suggests a motive behind his love of Joe, one that Joe himself has not presented (256). On two occasions (chs 11 and 16) the reader hears Jed's voice at least semidirectly in the letters that Joe inserts in his own narration. Here the reader is confronted in raw form with a rapturous, excited, fascinated love for another human being, a supreme confidence that the writer knows what the loved one feels and what he will do. Jed is as firm in his religious belief as he is in his belief that Joe truly loves him, and these beliefs do not waver even in the asylum (appendix 2). The sections in which Jed speaks are the exposure of a mind in perpetual ecstasy; they are meant to be both strangely moving and quite terrifying.

Clarissa and Jed are substantial psychological entities in their own right explored in some detail in the novel. But the primary focus of *Enduring Love* is on the narrator himself, on Joe. Indeed, the novel is, centrally, an analysis of a complex individual. Joe is a character who is deeply self-conscious. What he says and what he does are subjected to close analysis by himself; he is listening to and observing himself all the while. For example, after the ballooning accident he both acts and observes himself acting. "Like a self in a dream I was both first and third persons" (21). "I was in a soap opera. *Now he's talking to his woman.* It was intimacy, a tight two-shot" (23). In the London Library, his feeling of guilt and his sense that someone is following him are minutely analyzed by Joe himself (46). Such self-consciousness makes self-deceit more difficult. Rejected by Clarissa, pursued by Jed, Joe walks the dark, rainy London streets, past the homes of the wealthy. For a moment he indulges in the fancy that he is a poor outcast, but rapidly makes himself aware that this is a trick he is playing on his own feelings. At the same time, he puzzles over the image of the curtain that will eventually lead him to de Clérambault's syndrome and reflects on the intricate interweavings of mental processes in the brain (96). Self-examination and self-consciousness run throughout Joe's story. The novel gains its psychological focus to a considerable extent from this self-scrutiny.

What is the psychological portrait of Joe Rose that the novel provides? It is certainly elaborate, rich, and ambiguous. Joe is, first of all, the picture of a man driven by guilt—guilt for having let go of the rope in the ballooning accident and thus caused Logan's death.[7] Joe's insistence that he is *not* to blame is, perhaps, a little too strident (14). To make love with Clarissa afterward, he has to drive away the image of the dead man's home, wife, and children (39). This guilt pursues him throughout the novel. He realizes that he has visited Mrs. Logan in order to assert his guiltlessness (116). Returning to the scene of the accident, he imagines various figures coming to accuse him of some misdemeanor, although he is not sure what (128).

The second major component of Joe's psychological makeup (which overlaps with the first) is deep existential upheaval. The novel shows a character observing the collapse of his own mental and emotional world. The severe disturbance that Jed's mad love brings into Joe's life can be seen in his anguished, unspoken cry to Clarissa. "*Don't leave me here with my mind*, I thought. *Get them to let me out*" (61). "It was as if I had fallen through a crack in my own existence," he reflects, "down into another life, another set of sexual preferences, another past history and future" (71).

Above all, the fractures appear because Joe is a man who clings to order and control, but who has to face disorder and a frightening lack of control over his circumstances. His attachment to order and control is deep. Looking at the balloon as he and Clarissa walk together, he reflects with, one feels, a note of disapproval "that it was a precarious form of transport where the wind, rather than the pilot, set the course" (5). Joe is certainly not the type to go ballooning (although his own life is swept away by the strong gusts of Jed's love). His mind and character are marked by the "hundred feet or so of box-files" and "the little skyscraper of a hard disk drive" (98) in which he stores the information that may be useful to him in the future, and which, indeed, turns out to be so. He is a man who believes in archives, and whose own thought processes are compared by his lover (and by himself) to "calculations," to "double-entry book-keeping" (111). Once he has placed Jed's ailment within the borders of de Clérambault's syndrome, he feels relieved, delighted, almost happy (134). The frightening chaos of Jed's disorder (in the sense of disease, but also in the sense of the disruption he brings to Joe's world) is contained within the description of the disease and its possible development.

Joe's devotion to order and control is part of his worldview, and this worldview is a major part of the psychological focus of *Enduring*

Love. The novel takes a character (Joe) of a particular set of mind and presents him and it closely and with a degree of complexity and ambiguity. Joe is a character who is fact-oriented, materialist, rational, distrustful of emotions and what cannot be discussed logically, and extremely authoritative and confident in his pronouncements on the world. He is also a character who has a strong sense of failure and disappointment and is prone at times to irrational behavior and ways of thought.

Joe has a marked materialistic and rational side to his character. Right at the start of the novel he notes that he was unable to write powerful love letters to Clarissa, for "all that sincerity would permit me were the facts, and they seemed miraculous enough to me," the "facts" being that the beautiful Clarissa could love the unglamorous Joe (7). Throughout the novel, Joe views the world through the prism of material data. He assesses the percentage gradient of the sloping ground over which the balloon hangs (10–11); he calculates the mathematics of the failed rescue attempt ("if we assumed an average weight of sixty pounds each") (58). He thinks of Logan's death, and of death in general, in terms of current scientific terminology of the physical process of death and the "closing down of countless interrelated neural and bio-chemical exchanges" (25). Joe is a materialist. God has no place in his vision of the world. There is no controlling plan or agency, only physical processes. Eventually he abruptly rejects Jed's appeal that they pray together—"Because, my friend, no one's listening. There's no one up there" (29)—and he simply dismisses Clarissa's desire that Logan's death mean something (36). Jed writes that Joe's articles offend and sadden him because they are unremittingly materialist and rational, with no place for the divine, for Jed's or anyone else's God. Creation is a matter of physical, objectively observable processes, not God's work (145–46).

Joe is not just a materialist, but a rationalist as well. At least this is what Clarissa and Jed call him, and much of what one knows of him tends to suggest that he would be classed as such in most readers' minds. "You're so rational sometimes," Clarissa sighs in exasperation when Joe refuses to agree that Logan's death has some meaning (36). Jed hates Joe's "reason and logic" that stand (according to him) between Joe and a sense of the Christ within him (70). Joe himself acknowledges he has "a talent for clarity," an ability to make difficult experimental science and scientific theory understandable to a wide audience (79), while his observations on a number of phenomena, from babies' smiles to making love, have the lack of emotion and of vague feeling that are usually associated with rationalism (73–74, 172–73). "Information, foresight and careful calculation," are what are "needed" in life, according to Joe, not Clarissa's vague emotions and Jed's erotic and religious rapture (161).

In fact, in a philosophical sense Joe is not entirely a rationalist, but rather an empiricist. That is, he gives precedence to physical data that can be observed and calculated rather than to sequences of reasoned thought. After all, certain kinds of rational argument can support the existence of the divine, which for Joe would be empirically unacceptable. However, in other philosophical terms Joe's rejection of the divine (and his insistence that reason and calculation should be the basis for thought and action and that these are, in fact, the basis of human behavior) puts him within the category of rationalists.[8]

However that may be, Joe's worldview allows him to speak with very considerable confidence and authority, and this is a very important feature of his character. Joe speaks with forceful certainty about himself, about what happens to him, and about things in general. For example, of the ballooning accident he declares: "I know that if I had been uncontested leader the tragedy would not have happened" (11). "I'm not prepared to accept that it was me," he insists in answer to the question of who was responsible for Logan's death (14). This continues throughout the novel. After his quarrel with Clarissa he wants to return to her "not because I had behaved badly or was wrong, but because I was so obviously, incontrovertibly right, and she was simply mistaken" (98). When he visits the police for a second time after the shooting in the restaurant, he begins: "I might as well tell you straight away that I know what happened" (191). This confidence about self and what directly touches him is matched by an authority on more general matters. "There's never a moment's doubt or hesitation or admission of ignorance," Jed points out concerning Joe's writing (147), and Joe is certainly a man who lets you know his opinion on things. "Mostly we are good when it makes sense," he remarks in a manner that is typical of his way of speaking about the world (15).

Joe's language is that of authority. This can be noted in the apodictic (that is, in form assertive, completely certain) statements or rhetorical questions that mark his speech. But his vocabulary, too, is one that demands the reader's assent, a vocabulary of scientific fact and certainty. For example, Joe describes his feelings during the ballooning accident, using words like "barely a neuronal pulse later," "thoughts in which fear and instant calculations of logarithmic complexity were fused," and "less than one adrenally incensed heartbeat later" (14). One example may stand for many others. As they begin their sexual foreplay, Joe notes of Clarissa that "her hands were working across my buttocks towards my perineum" (36). Even

SCIENCE AND FICTIONS

concerning such an intimate act, Joe favors the language of the empirical sciences. This kind of authority of scientific discourse is embodied in the psychiatric journal article given in appendix 1 as well. (Jed's and Clarissa's language, in fact, does not substantially differ from Joe's, except with regard to the presence of scientific terminology in the narrator's discourse. Jed favors a religious, syntactically rather repetitive style, with a fondness for exclamations, while Clarissa writes a rather neutral, educated English. The relative social and educational homogeneity of character and milieu in the novel is reflected here. He and Clarissa and Joe speak similar languages, although in Jed's and Joe's cases with markedly different accents.)

So the picture the novel paints of Joe seems foursquare and solid—a rationalist, a materialist, a man of science who speaks with confidence and certainty. And, of course, Joe turns out to be right all along, about Jed, about his illness, about the danger he poses. But it is not as simple as that, and McEwan's psychological study of his narrator-protagonist is ambiguous. "There's no problem with Joe Rose," Jed writes ironically, mockingly. "His world is in place, everything fits, and all the problems are with Jed Parry" (146). Jed may, indeed, be a madman, but his irony is in place. Everything is not quite foursquare and stable with Joe Rose. Despite his success he is a man with a sense of failure. He is a recycler of others' ideas, not an original research scientist (79–80). Even with his confidence in his rationalist, empirical worldview, he suffers "a familiar disappointment" when the police point out that objectivity seems unattainable (196). Believing is seeing, he remarks on two occasions (131, 196). His worldview is not so well underpinned as he suggests elsewhere.

He may think of himself as a man of facts and science, and a skeptic about the value of the humanities, but he himself is capable

portrayal of its narrator and principal character. With regard to this strong psychological focus, two further aspects of the novel seem worth commenting on. The first is that, in terms of genre, *Enduring Love* is almost entirely a psychological study of its principal characters. Crime story and detective story elements are present, but these are finally of a fairly rudimentary kind. The intricacies of plot, the "who-dunnit" mystery aspects of much detective fiction are not really there in *Enduring Love*. Joe is a detective of sorts and there is some of the violence associated with crime novels, but these are subordinated to psychological portraiture.

The second striking feature of this novel's interest in psychology is that the social and historical aspects of characters' lives are almost completely ignored. It has been noted above that Joe, Clarissa, and Jed speak the same language (with different vocabularies, perhaps, but essentially the same social dialect). When Joe first meets Jed, he notes "a trace, or acknowledgment, of Cockney—a discarded past or an affectation" (26). British social class differences have traditionally been marked by language, especially phonology, and the reader learns from Jed himself that he is the only member of his family to get an education past the age of sixteen (104). However, the article in the *British Review of Psychiatry* does not note any social deprivation or conditioning in Jed's case (appendix 1), and Joe's main observation about Jed's speech has to do with his age rather than with social class (26). The social setting of the novel is very homogeneous. Apart from excursions to police stations, the world is that of libraries, radio producers, universities, good restaurants, and expensive apartments. Even Joe's encounter with the ex-hippies does not take him outside the middle classes (as Johnny B. Well points out, "Relative to the scene . . . these people are intellectuals" [206]). There is no reference to contemporary politics or to any historical or social forces that might have shaped characters' lives. They all live in a fairly well-off world, but this is in no way presented as a factor in their lives and fates. It is even quite difficult to date the novel's action. Joe's rare excursion into his own past gives no dates (80–81), and the reader gets a time of setting from a reference to Keats's upcoming two hundredth birthday (8), which sets the novel just before 1995. All this is striking in relation to the rest of McEwan's fiction. It is a return to the eerily insulated worlds of *The Cement Garden* and *The Comfort of Strangers* and a departure from the historically and socially focused worlds of *The Child in Time*, *The Innocent*, and *Black Dogs*.

"Its title, *Enduring Love*, explicitly announces McEwan's perennial romantic theme," notes Oliver Reynolds in his review of the novel in the *Times Literary Supplement*.[9] It is a novel not just about psychological states, but more specifically about that central psychological state: love. Love is, indeed, one of the novel's main focuses—largely pathological love or the pathology of love, but love nonetheless. There are four (slightly overlapping) pairs of lovers in the novel, and through them McEwan depicts the dangerous and valuable force of love and passion, and how love can break and be broken under pressure. The lovers are: Joe and Clarissa, Jed and Joe, Mrs. Logan and her dead husband, and Bonnie and the professor. The last two are part of the Logan subplot. The eminent professor has fallen in love and is having an affair with one of his students, thirty years younger than he and, as Joe acknowledges, very pretty in "a line of descent from Marilyn Monroe" (244). The professor (and Joe says he can understand his actions) will risk everything for his love for the silent, possibly stupid Bonnie (245, 248). Love makes one do strange things. It certainly drives Mrs. Logan to the brink of despair. She is convinced that her dead husband had a mistress (and there are reasonable grounds for thinking this), and she is obsessively concerned to find out who she is and how long the affair has been going on (124–26). As he observes her, Joe has a sense that he is watching in her "love, and the slow agony of its destruction" (121). Even the discovery that her husband is innocent brings no relief. "But who's going to forgive me?" she asks. "The only person who can is dead" (247).

The psychopathology of love is the central focus of McEwan's depiction of Jed's passion for Joe. The authors of the paper on Jed's case conclude with the observation that "the pathological extensions of love not only touch upon but overlap with normal experience, and it is not always easy to accept that one of our most valued experiences may merge into psychopathology" (259). The point about de Clérambault sufferers is that they are ecstatically in love with the object of their desires. This is borne out in what is seen of Jed's letters to Joe. They are alive with passion and a sense of the world's brightness and richness because of the love the writer feels. He sees the sunlight on a wall, the branches of a cherry tree; he feels the legs of an insect that crawls over his hand; he rejoices in his love; he covers five sheets of paper with his beloved's name (101–6). And the rapture will go on forever. But Jed's love is also sick. It can turn to violence and is quite immune to external proofs. Joe reflects that even if he did confess undying love for Jed, it would make no difference to the young lover. His love is really an absorption in himself, a terrible and dangerous solipsism. That this love is largely expressed in terms familiar from love poetry and cherished notions of what love is makes its pathological aspects all the more worrying.

If there is what might be called a healthy love in *Enduring Love*, it is in Joe and Clarissa's relationship. Theirs seems successful, warm, stable, the kind of love that should endure (170). Parts of what Joe tells us are hymns to companionableness, mutual emotional support, exchanges of ideas, and the physical pleasures of sex with a loved one (36–39, 171–73). In fact, appendix 1 reveals that they do come together again after their terrible experiences with Jed (258–59), but what the novel has shown is the desperate vulnerability of even the best of loves. Joe realizes the tremendous importance of love (121), but also its ambiguities (161) (is Clarissa glad to leave him?) and complexities (233–36) (you can be right, save your lover, and still have got it all wrong). Maybe, of course, Joe was lying all along. Maybe his and Clarissa's love was not so fine after all. But Clarissa does not suggest that this is so (233–36). Again, the novel is all the more frightening. A chance encounter can destroy even what is good; there does not have to be any rot in it already.

As critics have frequently noticed, love is one of McEwan's major themes. It is central in all his fiction, but how he presents it varies slightly from novel to novel. In *The Cement Garden*, love is finally redemptive; Jack and Julie's love, despite being incestuous, is a kind of glorious thing. In *The Comfort of Strangers* it is love's fragility that is stressed, as well as its extraordinary power. Colin and Mary, Robert and Caroline are deeply in love (even if those loves are flawed and ambiguous), but certainly Colin and Mary's sniffing out adventure leads to death and grief. Love is fragile, too, in *The Child in Time*. Stephen and Julie's marriage collapses in the face of their loss. But love is also redemptive; in the end they have another child and can begin once more. In *The Innocent* and in *Black Dogs*, this fragile yet redemptive quality of love is stressed again. Maria and Leonard cannot stay together, but their love has shaped their lives, and maybe in the end they will meet despite time and distance. June and Bernard cannot live together, but never divorce and remain in love till death and beyond. Bernard seeks his wife's face even after she is dead. The overall vision of love in *Enduring Love* is, however, altogether darker than in the previous novels, except perhaps in *The Comfort of Strangers*. It is central to the characters' lives but very fragile, and in some forms very dangerous and damaging. And redemptive? One does not see much hope of nonpathological love enduring and enriching characters' lives. What future do Bonnie and the professor have? Mrs. Logan's life will continue to be riddled with grief and guilt. All one knows of Joe and Clarissa in the future is a laconic sentence in a psychiatric paper. Only Jed is happy and transfigured in his love, and he is crazy and in an asylum.

Besides psychological portraiture and love, *Enduring Love* has one other major concern: that of knowledge. It is a kind of epistemological fiction, presenting and contrasting different kinds of knowledge and also considering both the limits and the possibilities of knowing the world.[10]

As has been noted above, Joe is an advocate of knowledge based on facts, the traditional empirical sciences (physics, biology, chemistry), traditional logic and reason. In addition, he has a strong sense of the possibilities of knowing the world through these. "It really helps to know," he insists to Clarissa about Jed's illness (159), and the mode of knowing he proposes is through the disciplines of psychology and psychiatry. This is very typical of his whole mental makeup. His narration bristles with allusions to and brief expositions of scientific ideas and theories, with material and empirically observable facts. His whole atheistic worldview is based on the authority of the traditional sciences and the sufficiency of the material world. The high value he puts on the knowledge the traditional empirical sciences can give him is well represented by his lines of box-files and his hard disk drive in his study (98) and by his relief when he discovers the details of de Clérambault's syndrome (134). He speaks with great authority in the confidence that the knowledge this way of understanding the world gives him is accurate and reliable.

But both Clarissa and Jed put forward other ways of knowing the world. Clarissa gets exasperated with Joe when he starts to analyze why babies smile in genetic, evolutionary, rational terms. No, he has not understood, she keeps repeating. She is talking about "love," not selfish survival mechanisms (75). Clarissa seems to value ill-defined emotions, that which can not be dissected logically. In her letter to Joe she argues that he was right about Jed, but somehow emotionally wrong in the way he went about the whole matter (235). If Clarissa speaks with a certain hesitancy about things (for example, about Logan's death [35–36]), Jed not only puts forward a radically different way of knowing the world from Joe's, but also speaks of things with a tremendous confidence that matches that of the object of his desire. As one has seen, he is a believer with a vague, but powerful, metaphysical view of the world. Emotions, feelings, and inspiration are all to him; material facts are nothing. No matter how often Joe says to him that he does not love him, Jed will continue to believe that he does. For him, Joe's materialism, his rationalism, his science are the bars of his "little cage of reason"

(144), from which Jed wishes to set his beloved free. Joe argues that Jed is immune to any proof beyond his own feelings and convictions, a fantasist and solipsist who would be quite incapable of giving an account of events or his feelings that would be lucid to others (153–58, 163–64, 229). It is worth noting that this other way of knowing is partly associated with women. Clarissa is female, and Jed, for part of the novel, wears his hair in a ponytail (26). It is also worth emphasizing that this kind of knowledge is finally seen as inadequate and dangerous in *Enduring Love*. Mars-Jones acidly comments that "McEwan's emotional engagement with feminism is less deferent than once it was."[11] Certainly, his valuation of men's and women's ways of seeing the world is not the same as it is in *Or Shall We Die?*, *The Child in Time*, or *Black Dogs*.

The novel presents different kinds of knowledge, both of which give their possessors considerable certainty. (Joe's language is shot through with the authority of science, Jed's with the authority of religious terminology.) But what the novel also shows is that knowledge is (like love) a rather fragile thing, difficult to get and, indeed, rather unstable. An atmosphere of epistemological uncertainty bedevils the world of *Enduring Love*. For one thing, scientific knowledge is itself scarcely as firm and solid as it might be, and Joe knows this. He notes that biologists and evolutionary psychologists are calling the postwar consensual model of the social sciences into question, with their stress on genetic inheritance rather than environmental factors in individual development (73–74). Presumably, the knowledge based on the now outdated consensual model was firm and solid, but now is not. "Believing is seeing," Joe quotes a research colleague as saying (131, 196). Scientific knowledge can be as much a matter of wishful thinking as Jed's passion.

There are a number of examples of dubious certainty and uncertainty in the novel. Jed is convinced Joe loves him; he does not. Mrs. Logan is convinced her husband is an adulterer; he is not. The ex-hippies Joe meets reel off pseudoeducated banalities about the environment as if they were gospel (213–14). There are also a number of moments of deep uncertainty in the novel. Does Jed really exist, wonders Clarissa, or at least in the form Joe gives him (90)? Why is Joe's and Jed's handwriting so similar, she wonders (108)? For a short time, at least, the reader, too, perhaps wonders. Is Joe making all this up? Is Jed some kind of projection of his guilt, a spirit, a real figure, called up to punish himself? The reader is in suspense for part of the novel, not knowing for sure quite what is going on. The climax of this strand in the story takes place in the police station after the shooting in the restaurant (193–98). The policeman who takes statements from the witnesses gives a weary list of the subjects on which the witnesses cannot agree. It is significant that Joe responds to the policeman's list, which suggests that knowledge is a fairly dubious concept altogether, with a sense of "familiar disappointment" (196). Objectivity and "disinterested truth" are hard to get at, but—the conclusion of his reflection here is important too—that does not make it less admirable to try, even though "it couldn't save us from ourselves" (196).

In the end, as the reader looks back at the novel, he/she is confronted with four possibilities related to the subject of knowledge. These are as follows. First, Joe is right. Facts are facts, and scientific knowledge will steer one best through the maze of human life. Second, Joe is an outright liar, and the narration is an extensive piece of self-justification to conceal or fictionalize the way he has made a mess of his relationships with Jed and Clarissa. Third, all forms of knowledge are equal—Jed's metaphysical ecstasy, Clarissa's ill-defined feelings, Joe's traditional scientific knowledge. Or fourth, knowledge is an uncertain thing, difficult to achieve, subject to revision, but is attainable, and the best way to it is through Joe's rationalism, materialism, and traditional science (although that way is not going to make him popular with his lover, even if he does save her from a madman). The novel comes out on the side of the last possibility. Joe may be frustrating to Clarissa, but—barring the possibility that the whole novel is meant to be read as an extensive piece of lying—his stubborn rationality is the best bet in the chaos of human impulses.

Other chapters in this study have suggested that McEwan has certain metafictional concerns in his novels. This is also true of *Enduring Love*, and it is a concern that intertwines with the epistemological interests noted above. In his *Times Literary Supplement* review Reynolds observes that "the opening sentence is one of a number that proclaims a self-aware narrative, a story as experiment, one where the telling will distance us from what is told."[12] As in McEwan's first two novels, there are a number of points in the novel where one's attention is drawn to the text of the novel as text. Unlike in *The Cement Garden* or *The Comfort of Strangers*, however, this is not achieved through language. Joe's language, like Jeremy's in *Black Dogs*, seems highly probable. Someone like him would speak that way. But there are frequent reminders by other means that one is encountering a fictional text when one reads. "The beginning is simple to mark," Joe declares in the first sentence, indicating that this is a narrative with a point of commencement, a story with a beginning. There are a number of other points where the madeness of the narrative is brought before the reader's eyes—"Let me freeze the frame," Joe says at one point (12); "Best to slow down," declares the narrator as self-conscious narrator (19). He makes a self-advertising switch of point of view in chapter 9; he concludes the climax of the action by telling you it is a climax (231).

But also, as in some of McEwan's earlier novels, there is an examination of the roles narratives, stories, and fictions play in characters' (and, by extension, readers') lives. As was noted above, there is a strong emphasis in *Enduring Love* on the explanations and interpretations of events people give, and how untrustworthy and partial many of them are. Throughout the novel, too, characters make up stories to explain things, to justify themselves, to make life bearable. Joe and Clarissa work hard at converting the horror of the ballooning accident into a tolerable narrative (33–34). Joe is curious about Jed because he realizes he will need more detail about his persecutor if he is to turn the whole thing into a good story for his friends (63). Mrs. Logan sees herself as disturbing to others because her questions about her husband "don't fit the story" (121). She herself, of course, concocts one to explain the scarf and the picnic things in her husband's car. According to Jed, Joe has made up a "story" running throughout his articles, a story that denies God (144–45). Joe sees Jed as making up a "story" too, one that will allow him to believe Joe will leave Clarissa and come to him (154). Toward the end of the novel, Clarissa talks to Joe of all they have been through together recently as a "story," the end of which she wishes to see (237).

Characters make stories constantly, and the novel stresses the limits of these stories (thus, metafiction connects with concerns about knowledge). Jed's story of Joe's loving him is nonsense. Mrs. Logan's narrative of her husband's adultery is a fiction. Joe simply rejects some of the details of Clarissa's version of events (239–40). The police officer who takes Joe's first call has to process his "private narrative" into a bureaucratic mold (78). Film narratives lie, according to Joe, about the moments after climactic events (231), and, of course, none of the witnesses can quite agree about what happened in the restaurant (193–98). Any story is a partial retelling, limited and distorting, of events. One of the most striking examples of this comes in appendix 1, in which the events of the novel are retold in a completely different language, that of the scholarly, psychiatric paper. Jed's insane certainty becomes "a well-encapsulated delusional system" (255), and the beautiful, much-loved Clarissa becomes Joe's "common-law wife" (254). Knowledge is embodied in stories, and these stories are seen to be limited in a variety of ways. Either the authors deliberately distort, as it seems Jed does, or just get things wrong through inattention and human frailty or through the particular discourse they employ. But that does not mean that McEwan is arguing all stories are equal; quite the reverse. For all the reservations the reader may have about Joe's vision of the world and the makeup of his mind, he is righter than the rest and wins in the end.

Enduring Love is an intriguing story, an intricate, psychological novel, a dark commentary on love's fragility, an examination of the limits and possibilities of knowledge, and a sophisticated metafictional piece. In this, his sixth novel, McEwan seems, indeed, to have become a very substantial writer.

CHAPTER NINE

Other Works
Screenplays, the Oratorio, Children's Fiction, and *Amsterdam*

McEwan has not limited himself only to novels and short fiction, but has tried writing for other media. His output includes plays for television, film scripts, and the text for an oratorio. In addition, he has written two pieces of fiction for children. Although *Amsterdam* (1998) is a novel (if a very short one), it is included in this chapter because it does not really merit a chapter on its own. It does, however, show interesting links with McEwan's work in other media, especially with the socially critical, sour vision of the world in the screenplay *The Ploughman's Lunch*.

It must be noted from the start that when it comes to McEwan's work in other media, the literary critic is confronted with certain problems. Television plays, a film script, and an oratorio are not novels or short stories. A whole range of visual and auditory elements comes into play that is lacking in prose fiction. These surely require a specialized terminology and approach that are different from those of literary analysis. However, this chapter treats the screenplays and oratorio as written texts on the grounds that the readers of this study are most likely to come across them as such. (Indeed, one of the TV plays, *Solid Geometry*, was never completed and does not exist as a film.) One must remember, nevertheless, that a key component of the oratorio *Or Shall We Die?* (and, indeed, the key element) is Michael Berkeley's music, while *The Ploughman's Lunch*, as a whole, is shaped by Richard Eyre's direction and the very distinguished acting of Jonathan Pryce, Rosemary Harris, and Frank Finlay.

Other Media

McEwan's work in media other than written prose includes three plays for television, *Jack Flea's Birthday Celebration* (1976), *Solid Geometry* (1979), and *The Imitation Game* (1980), and the oratorio *Or Shall We Die?* (1983). *Jack Flea's Birthday Celebration* strongly echoes the plays of Harold Pinter with their tense family conflicts and striking images of extreme psychological states. McEwan says that his intention in this play was to break the "conventions" of TV's dominant "naturalism," but, although the play does present certain psychological situations that verge on the pathological—Ruth, for example, spoonfeeds her lover David at one point—nothing in the text really breaks the laws of probability or physical possibility.[1] The play was broadcast by the BBC in 1976.

Solid Geometry is a faithful adaptation of McEwan's story of the same name from *First Love, Last Rites*. The BBC stopped production of the film version, probably because it was felt that the penis preserved in formaldehyde that stands on the protagonist's desk for much of the play would cause public offense. *The Imitation Game* was, however, made successfully into a TV film and broadcast by the BBC in 1980. It is set in England in 1940 and centers on the experiences of the nineteen-year-old Cathy Raine. The lively protagonist encounters varieties of male nastiness, institutional and personal. Women's place, even in this time of national emergency, is in mindless work or cleaning floors, and if any woman gets above her station, she is punished. McEwan published all three TV plays in one volume in 1981.

Or Shall We Die? is an oratorio commissioned from McEwan and the composer Michael Berkeley by the London Symphony Orchestra with funds provided by the Arts Council of Great Britain (the British Government's agency for arts sponsorship). It was first performed at the Royal Festival Hall in London in 1983. An oratorio is a traditional, semidramatic musical composition, in the past frequently based on a biblical subject, which is performed by a choir with soloists and a full orchestra, without costumes, action, or scenery. There is little narrative element in McEwan's text, which expresses deep unease at what the author sees as the danger to the world of nuclear weapons and of uncontrolled male-dominated science and technology. These are contrasted with a nurturing, life-giving, healing female spirit. The text is centered around a Man's and a Woman's voice, and the Woman's sums up its didactic purpose in the question "Shall there be womanly times, or shall we die?" *The Ploughman's Lunch* is a full-length feature film, first given general release in Britain in 1983 and in the U.S. in 1984. It is set in the (then) contemporary world of early 1980s Britain and revolves around the main character's selling out to what is presented as the meretricious ethos of Mrs. Thatcher's Britain.

Certain features of all these texts stand out. Several are psychological studies; several are directly concerned with historical and social subjects; and two at least show a strong feminist purpose. They are deeply connected with McEwan's work as a whole.

Jack Flea's Birthday Celebration and *Solid Geometry* show the kind of concern with psychological states that is familiar from the short stories written at approximately the same time. *Solid Geometry* presents in dramatic form the same disintegrating marriage, the same bitter tension between male and female that are the subjects of the short story of the same name. Family tensions, the jealousy of the mother, the desire on the part of the older female lover to show that David is hers, David's own complex desires to resist these powerful women and yet to give in to them at the same time—these are the psychological focuses of *Jack Flea's Birthday Celebration*. It ends with an image of confinement and control that could come straight out of *First Love, Last Rites* or *In between the Sheets*. Psychological states, too, form a central concern in *The Imitation Game*. Cathy's deep frustration in her male-dominated world, her moving attempts to break through the codes and barriers of her environment, the young mathematician's despair at his own impotence, and the loathing and blaming of the woman that ensues are all memorably presented in the text. Similarly, although his fate is shaped by social and historical forces, too, Penfield's psychological portrait in *The Ploughman's Lunch*—his uneasy desire to gain access to the British establishment, his burnt-out cynicism yet longing for the lovely Susan—is memorably dark.

Both *The Imitation Game* and *The Ploughman's Lunch* are seen by McEwan himself as attempts to broaden the focus of his fiction from introverted psychological portraiture to the historical and the social.[2] Although, as has been suggested in chapters 2 to 4, one can exaggerate the separation of characters and situations in McEwan's early fiction from the wider world, it is true that the social and the political do not play a major role in "Last Day of Summer" or *The Cement Garden*, for example. This is clearly not the case in *The Imitation Game* and *The Ploughman's Lunch*, in which the primary focus is on how characters' fates are shaped by their political and historical circumstances. In *The Imitation Game* Cathy's life is formed by World War II and her involvement in the top-secret

Bletchley codebreaking project. In *The Ploughman's Lunch* James Penfield rewrites the history of Britain's invasion of Egypt in 1956 to fit in with a new political and national order. Recalling the old wounds of Suez surely asks the viewer or reader to wonder about the bombast associated with the Falklands/Malvinas War of 1982. Penfield himself is meant to be an example of what McEwan sees as the corrupt self-interest and self-delusions of early 1980s Britain. The unpalatable final image of him at his mother's funeral, glancing at his watch, is an austere, concise commentary on the political and moral life of the country (and one that McEwan develops later in *The Child in Time* and in *Amsterdam*).

One broad social issue that is never far from the heart of McEwan's novels and short stories (except *Amsterdam* and the work for children) is that of male-female relations of power, and differences in psychological makeup and social conditioning that help to shape these. This is true in a short story like "Homemade" or "Pornography," as it is in novels such as *The Comfort of Strangers* or *Black Dogs*. *The Imitation Game* addresses the feminist concern of how women have been excluded from important areas of human activity. Cathy is relegated to washing floors and serving tea, and any attempt to cross the border that the male world imposes on her leads to punishment. In *The Ploughman's Lunch* the protagonist Penfield uses Ann Barrington and ignores the women from the anti-nuclear weapons peace camp whom he encounters. One is meant to applaud when Susan ditches him for his friend. Although neither Ann nor Susan provides a voice against the selfishness and silliness of early 1980s Britain, the women from the peace camp do. This is a voice that is repeated in *Or Shall We Die?* Men will destroy the world; women will save it. Men are linear, Newtonian exploiters of the natural world; women are the source of life and healing, with a much less absolutist and controlling set of mind. The critic Adam Mars-Jones describes this aspect of McEwan's work as advocating "certain values, particularly the decommissioning of the male ego in favor of a new personality attuned to women and children."[3] The Woman's voice in *Or Shall We Die?* certainly speaks for a type of feminist agenda, and one that is a crucial aspect of *The Child in Time* and *Black Dogs.*

Children's Fiction

The child and the adolescent are obviously very important figures in McEwan's fiction. Several short stories and *The Cement Garden* have children as their central characters. *The Child in Time* is also about a child, but about one who is absent for most of the text, while *Black Dogs* starts off with the narrator's adolescence, and both his abused sister and the child he rescues in the French restaurant are victims of a human wickedness that is central to the novel. But although there are several important children in McEwan's writing, most of his work is not written for children. *Rose Blanche* (1985) and *The Daydreamer* (1994) are exceptions.

McEwan's contribution to the picture book *Rose Blanche* is quite small. His text, based on a story by Christophe Gallaz, is really just an adjunct to the at times very powerful and intricate pictures of Roberto Innocenti depicting war and its cruelties. *The Daydreamer*, however, is all McEwan's, and is in itself an interesting text that relates closely to his adult fiction. In his Preface to *The Daydreamer*, McEwan notes that the stories in this collection are about imagination and transformation.[4] Individual chapters/stories recount the adventures of Peter Fortune, who starts the volume as a ten-year-old and ends it at twelve. In the course of these stories he is attacked by his sister's malevolent doll, is changed into an aging tomcat and a baby, makes his family vanish, defeats a bully, captures a thief, and becomes an adult for a short time. In most of these adventures, he learns something important: fear, the power of a sense of injustice, bravery, his need for his family, and openness to others' lives and experiences. In most of the stories Peter passes from a world where normal rules apply (you can't get inside a cat's fur, for example) to one where many things are possible (vanishing cream will make people and things disappear). The reader is meant to understand that the transformations and adventures are largely Peter's daydreams (the title alone indicates this), although the movement from one world to the next is fairly seamless.

The Daydreamer is, in part, a celebration of childhood as a state of partial freedom and anarchy. Peter can move from an everyday world of school and family holidays to a world of magical transformations in which traditional rules no longer apply. This is sometimes a frightening world (for example, his sister's Bad Doll is very nasty), but it is also a world of excitement, freedom from limitation, and fascinating experiences. In this respect *The Daydreamer* bears some relation to the stories of childhood in *First Love, Last Rites*. In addition, the element of defamiliarization noted with regard to those early stories is echoed in *The Daydreamer*. Peter learns to see the world through a baby's eyes and taste buds (120), and he himself observes adults from a twelve-year-old's perspective in a way that is cleverly disorienting and yet recognizable for the adult reader (131, 136). When he is transformed into an adult, he sees adult experience with a disturbing freshness.

But technically the novel goes out of its way not to disturb. Like McEwan's early short stories, the chapters of *The Daydreamer*

Lunch. The novel certainly recalls his previous work. The question of the fallibility of memory and perception that is raised when Clive attends a police identity parade echoes a similar incident in *Enduring Love*, while the transvestism that is the central agent of the action touches on material in the early story "Disguises" and in *The Comfort of Strangers*.[6] *Amsterdam* has a relatively complex story material. Set in the mid-1990s, it centers on the moral dilemmas confronting two successful, middle-aged friends, a composer and a newspaper editor. One of these dilemmas involves a decision whether to publish photographs that reveal an eminent Conservative Party politician to be a transvestite. The novel ends with each of the two friends, now bitter enemies, arranging the other's death.

The novel's reception has been, as ever, quite mixed, many critics praising its skill and acute commentary on part of contemporary British life, others finding the piece lightweight and lacking in substance. In general terms, the reviews divide as follows: the *Guardian* (5 Sept. 1998), the *Daily Express* (12 Sept. 1998), the *Independent on Sunday* (13 Sept. 1998), the *Daily Telegraph* (19 Sept. 1998), the *Sunday Telegraph* (13 Sept. 1998), and the *Sunday Times* (13 Sept. 1998) say the novel is good; the *Mail on Sunday* (13 Sept. 1998), the *Times* (19 Sept. 1998), the *Daily Mail* (9 Oct. 1998), and Anita Brookner in the *Spectator* (12 Sept. 1998) have their reservations. *Amsterdam*, however, was awarded the Booker Prize for fiction in 1998. After having two previous novels shortlisted and then not win (*The Comfort of Strangers* and *Black Dogs*), McEwan at last received this prestigious literary prize.

In his comments on the state of the novel in 1978, McEwan is critical of what he sees as the "good, well-made English novel" that "is still typically one which is carefully attuned to and minutely observant of the nuances of class and the niceties of sexual behavior. Its social and political judgments are instinctively conservative."[7] One could ask to what extent *Amsterdam* is such a novel, written and published some twenty years after McEwan was so critical of this kind of fiction. Certainly, as with the short stories and *The Daydreamer* and *Enduring Love*, *Amsterdam* is steeped in nineteenth-century and conservative twentieth-century novelistic tradition. Narration is omniscient. The narrator expresses himself in educated and authoritative, but far from baroquely self-advertising, language. At the funeral that opens the novel he concisely fills in the background to the dead woman's relationship with the protagonists Clive and Vernon (4–5). As Clive travels north by train, the narrator tells us what he does not see (71). He even begins one chapter with the authoritative and all-knowing "What actually happened was this. . . ." (73), and he allows himself universalizing utterances like "It can happen sometimes with those who brood on an injustice, that a taste for revenge can usually combine with a sense of obligation" (162). The narration switches point of view with the ease of a mid-nineteenth-century British novel. The narrative, too, is in this tradition: linear, logical, chronological. It even has elements of suspense: what is in the photographs George gives Vernon? (60–61); what do Clive and Vernon argue about? (67); what does Clive witness on the hills (94–95)? If the double murder in *Amsterdam* is signaled clearly very early in the text so as to make the ending predictable, there is enough suspense in the other parts of the novel. There is good traditional "plotting" in *Amsterdam*. The manner in which Conservative Party Central Office defeats Vernon provides a clever twist to the action (134–36). There is even a cunning subplot in which poor Vernon is outmaneuvered by one of his subordinates (119–20). And the whole novel comes to a satisfying conclusion, the two compromised friends punished for their hubris and greed.

Amsterdam, like much of McEwan's work, has strong elements of the psychological novel, that traditional genre in British fiction. Extensive sections of free indirect thought (in the form of indirect internal speech, but without any "he said that/he thought that"), which at times gets very close to free direct thought, set out the principal characters' emotions, worries, jealousies, doubts, and grandiose plans. For example, when early in the novel Clive observes Garmony, the thoughts are Clive's, not the narrator's, and they are given (allowing for the shifts to indirect discourse demanded by English) in approximations to his internal speech (16–17). As the novel proceeds, the reader enters the minds of the two protagonists and some other characters, too, and follows their moods, uncertainties, and intimations of mortality and immortality. If there is a certain insubstantiality about the characters, perhaps that is intentional on the author's part. To some extent they are nonentities, men taken up by their careers and material success and in a sense absorbed by that. Vernon actually has a sense that his personality has been "infinitely diluted," scattered among the hundreds of demands on his time and attention that his job as a newspaper editor makes (31–32). In any case, both Clive and Vernon feel themselves dying slowly. Clive's left hand starts to go dead on him (26–27); Vernon thinks the right side of his brain has already died (33–34, 41). A certain absence and vagueness in character might be appropriate. Indeed, lack of information about Clive's and Vernon's family backgrounds may make a telling point about these characters. They are men who have made it into the ranks of the British establishment. Their background is now irrelevant, as Penfield in *The Ploughman's Lunch* would like to

action of the text. The Conservative politician who stands for traditional family values and rigid social and penal codes is a closet
cross-dresser. Quality newspapers are to be dumbed down for the
cause of greater circulation figures. The aging, self-absorbed,
slightly inert protagonists choose self-interest over decency and
moral conduct. They also have outrageous delusions of grandeur,
Clive seeing himself as a latter-day Beethoven (143) and Vernon as
one of the great newspaper editors of his day (184–85). It is notable
that they relive these dreams of greatness as they drift off into
drugged unconsciousness before their fatal injections (183–84). A
whole generation (or at least its men, for there are almost no women
in this novel) within an important section of society is being mocked
in Clive's and Vernon's moral shabbiness and delusive self-esteem.

   Amsterdam, then, is part psychological novel and part social
satire. It is also, in part, a moral fable (rather like the chapters of *The
Daydreamer*). *Amsterdam* has the briefness, the relatively simple
characters, the clear moral and social dilemmas that are associated
with the genre. Clive and Vernon are each confronted with a moral
dilemma, and each makes a disastrous decision. Clive's moral
dilemma is simpler. On balance, his symphony cannot outweigh the
imperative to try to interrupt a rape. Vernon's dilemma is more complex. Garmony is a nasty piece of work who might well make the
world worse. But the reader suspects that this is finally a secondary
reason for Vernon's deciding to publish the pictures; the primary
one is a desire to save his own career by raising his paper's circulation. And for their shabbiness and worse, Vernon and Clive are duly
punished—fired, disgraced, ridiculed, ultimately the victims of each
other's pique. The moral could scarcely be clearer if the narrator set
it out: "Thus perish the hollow men." Alas, one cannot say that the

good are rewarded in *Amsterdam*, because there are no good. The only possibly admirable character is Garmony's surgeon wife, Ruth, but even she colludes with the Conservative Party media manipulators as her public service is used as a political weapon (131–36). The police fake their evidence (166–68); the critic who mocks Clive's music and Vernon's moral stature visits a pedophile brothel (179–80). The men who come out on top are as corrupt as the losers: Frank Dibben at *The Judge* and the pompous George. The world of the great and the good is a foul place in *Amsterdam*. For all that some of the wicked get their comeuppance, perhaps this novel is not as far from the amoral world of the early short stories and *The Cement Garden* as it might appear.

NOTES

Chapter 1—Understanding Ian McEwan

1. Ian Hamilton, "Points of Departure," *New Review* 5 (autumn 1978): 9.

2. Ian McEwan, introduction, *The Ploughman's Lunch* (London: Methuen, 1985), v.

3. Hamilton, "Points of Departure," 9.

4. Ibid., 15.

5. Jason Cowley, "Portrait: Ian McEwan," *Prospect* (Dec. 1998): 44.

6. Hamilton, "Points of Departure," 16.

7. Andrew Billen, "A Goodbye to Gore," *Observer Magazine,* 14 June 1992, 30.

8. Cowley, "Portrait: Ian McEwan," 43–44.

9. Ibid., 44.

10. Kiernan Ryan, *Ian McEwan,* Writers and Their Work, ed. Isobel Armstrong (Plymouth, U.K.: Northcote House/The British Council, 1994), 2. A very similar view underlies Jack Slay, Jr., *Ian McEwan*, (New York: Twayne Publishers, 1996), 34, 115.

11. Ryan, "Ian McEwan," 4–5.

12. McEwan, introduction, *The Imitation Game: Three Plays for Television* (London: Cape, 1981), 16.

13. John Haffenden, *Novelists in Interview* (London and New York: Methuen, 1985), 173.

14. A number of critics would endorse this summary. See, for example, Linda Hutcheon, "Historiographic Metafiction," in *Metafiction,* ed. Mark Currie (London and New York: Longman, 1995), 71–91. For U.S. examples (and influences?) in the field of metafiction, see Robert Scholes's well-known essay "Metafiction," reprinted in the same anthology (21–38).

15. McEwan, "The State of Fiction: A Symposium," *New Review* 5 (summer 1978): 51.

16. Adam Mars-Jones, *Venus Envy*, Chatto Counterblasts (London: Chatto and Windus, 1990), 24, 27–28, 31–32.

17. Cowley, "Portrait: Ian McEwan," 44.

Chapter 2—The Short Stories: *First Love, Last Rites* and *In between the Sheets*

1. Haffenden, *Novelists in Interview* (London and New York: Methuen, 1983), 189–190. The interview with McEwan is on pages 168 to 190.

2. Slay, *Ian McEwan,* 9–34, 51–71.

3. Cowley, "Portrait: Ian McEwan," 45.

4. The following reviews deal with *First Love, Last Rites* or *In between the Sheets:* Neil Schmitz, no title, *Partisan Review* 43, (1976): 646; William Abrahams, "A Matter of Small Moment," *Sewanee Review* 85, no. 1 (winter 1977): 111–115; Hermione Lee, "Shock Horror," *New Statesman,* 20 Jan. 1978, 86–87; Hermione Lee, no title, *Observer,* 17 Dec. 1978, 36; Julian Moynahan, "In an Advanced Modern Manner," *New York Times Book Review,* 26 Aug. 1979, 9, 20; Caroline Blackwood, "De Gustibus," *Times Literary Supplement,* 20 Jan. 1978, 53.

5. Both Hamilton and Ricks make this obvious in their interviews: Hamilton, "Points of Departure," 9–21, and Christopher Ricks, "Adolescence and After: An Interview with Ian McEwan," *The Listener,* 12 Apr. 1979, 526–27.

6. McEwan, *First Love, Last Rites* (New York: Vintage, 1994), 17. All references in parentheses are to this edition.

7. McEwan, *In between the Sheets* (New York: Vintage, 1994), 38. All references in parentheses are to this edition.

8. Ricks, "Adolescence and After," 526.

9. Kiernan Ryan comments on McEwan's fondness for the alienated and the outsider in his perceptive study *Ian McEwan,* ch. 2.

10. Moynahan, "Modern Manner," 9.

11. Hamilton, "Points of Departure," 17–18. In a recently published talk on Borges's fiction, McEwan states, with respect to texts by Jorge Luis Borges, that "Solid Geometry" is "part pastiche, part homage, part plagiarism." See Martin Amis and McEwan, "The Fiction of Jorge Luis Borges," *Areté* 2 (2000): 112.

12. This issue is raised by both Ricks and Haffenden in their interviews with McEwan (see note 5 above). The author professes himself rather bemused by readers' shocked reactions to his short stories. "Reviewers seemed to be fixated by things that weren't central," he says to Haffenden (172).

13. Schmitz, 646.

14. Cowley, "Portrait: Ian McEwan," 45.

15. Viktor Shklovsky, "Art as Technique," in *Russian Formalist Criticism: Four Essays,* trans. Lee T. Lemon and Marion J. Reis (Lincoln: University of Nebraska Press, 1965), 12. See also pp. 13–18.

16. Slay, *Ian McEwan,* 9–13.

17. Ryan, *Ian McEwan,* 11. Subsequently, however, he does suggest there is an underlying moral purpose in *In between the Sheets* (14).

18. Slay, *Ian McEwan,* 31–32.

Chapter 3—Fiction and Evil (I): *The Cement Garden*

1. The following reviews or articles deal with *The Cement Garden:* Wolfgang Wicht, "Ian McEwan: *Der Zementgarten,*" *Weimarer Beiträge* 36 (1990): 1146–56 (1148); Gérard Klaus, "Le monstreux et la dialectique du pur et de l'impur dans *The Cement Garden* de Ian McEwan," in *Le monstreux dans la littérature et la pensée anglaises,* ed. Nadia J. Rigaud (Aix-en-Provence: Université de Provence, 1985), 239–49 (243); Robert Towers, "In Extremis," *The New York Review of Books,* 8 March 1979, 8; Paul Ableman, "Regressive," *Spectator,* 30 Sept. 1978, 23–24; Blake

Morrison, "Paying Cellarage," *Times Literary Supplement,* 29 Sept. 1978, 1077.

2. Wicht, "Von *David Copperfield* zu Ian McEwans *The Cement Garden:* Veränderungen im Diskurs der Ich-Erzähler," *Zeitschrift fur Anglistik und Amerikanistik* 36, no. 4 (1988): 309, 311–12.

3. McEwan, *The Cement Garden* (New York: Vintage, 1994), 22–23. Page references in parentheses are to this edition.

4. Abelman, "Regressive," 23; Anthony Thwaite, "How to Keep Mum," *Observer,* 1 Oct. 1978, 33.

5. Hermione Lee, "First Rites," *New Statesman,* 29 Sept. 1978, 416.

6. Klaus, "Le monstreux," 245; Max Duperray, "L'étranger dans le contexte post-moderniste: *The Comfort of Strangers* d'Ian McEwan," in *L'étranger dans la littérature et la pensée anglaises* (Aix-en-Provence: Université de Provence, 1989), 429.

7. The "Condition-of-England" novel is the name given to a number of important and popular British novels of the 1840s and 1850s that directly address contemporary social and political problems. Dickens's *Hard Times* (1854) is an example of this type of novel. The phrase "Condition of England" comes from Thomas Carlyle's essay "Chartism" (1839).

Chapter 4—Fiction and Evil (II): *The Comfort of Strangers*

1. The following reviews deal with *The Comfort of Strangers:* Anthony Thwaite, "Ill-Met by Moonlight," *Observer,* 11 Oct. 1981, 33; J. R. Banks, "A Gondola Named Desire," *Critical Quarterly* 24, no. 2 (1982): 27–31; Christopher Ricks, "Playing with Terror," *London Review of Books,* 21 Jan.–3 Feb. 1982, 13–14; Richard P. Brickner, "Traveling in Peril," *New York Times Book Review,* 5 July 1981, 7; James Campbell, "Dreams of Pain," *New Statesman,* 9 Oct. 1981, 22–23; Lewis Jones, "More Filth," *Spectator,* 24 Oct. 1981, 23–24.

2. McEwan, *The Comfort of Strangers* (New York: Vintage, 1994), 9. Page references in parentheses are to this edition.

3. Ricks, "Playing with Terror," 13–14.

4. For the original, see John Ruskin's *The Stones of Venice* (1853), vol. 2, ch. 4, quoted in *Ruskin Today,* ed. Kenneth Clark (New York: Holt, Reinhart and Winston, 1964), 335–36.

5. Henry James, "Venice," in *Collected Travel Writings: The Continent,* (New York: Literary Classics of the United States, 1993), 287, 290.

6. Banks, "A Gondola"; Max Duperray, "L'étranger dans le contexte post-moderniste," 291–306; Ricks, "Playing with Terror."

7. Thomas Mann, *Der Tod in Venedig und andere Erzählungen* (Frankfurt am Main: Fischer Taschenbuch Verlag, 1954), 56–57. Page references in parentheses are to this edition.

8. All translations of Thomas Mann are mine.

9. Hamilton, "Points of Departure," 15.

10. Duperray, "L'étranger dans le contexte post-moderniste," 296–97.

11. See note 4 above.

12. See, for example, Bernard Bergonzi, *The Situation of the Novel* (London: Macmillan, 1979), 56; Alastair Fowler, *A History of English Literature: Forms and Kinds from the Middle Ages to the Present* (Oxford: Basil Blackwell, 1987), 364.

Chapter 5—Change, Dystopia, and the Way Out: *The Child in Time*

1. Brian Martin, "Looking Back to the Future," *Spectator,* 10 Oct. 1987, 40.

2. Slay, *Ian McEwan,* 115. The following are reviews of *The Child in Time:* Judy Cooke, "Time Stands Still," *Listener,* 17 Sept. 1987, 24; Boyd Tonkin, "In at the Birth," *New Statesman,* 18 Sept. 1987, 28; Gabriele Annan, "Worriers," *New York Review of Books,* 4 Feb. 1988, 17–19.

3. Michael Neve, "Possible Futures," *Times Literary Supplement,* 4 Sept. 1987, 947. See also Martin, "Looking Back," 40; Cooke, "Time Stands Still," 24; and Slay, *Ian McEwan,* 115.

4. Nicholas Spice, "Thatchershaft," *London Review of Books,* 1 Oct. 1987, 8–9. See also Annan, "Worriers," 19.

5. Mars-Jones, *Venus Envy,* 24, 27–28, 31–32. This is also noted by Neve (947), who, like Mars-Jones, discusses the novel's conclusion in terms of the cultural practice of *couvade,* whereby the male partner of a woman about to give birth simulates her experience and appropriates the birth.

6. Mars-Jones, *Venus Envy,* 33.

7. McEwan, *The Child in Time* (New York: Anchor Books, 1999), 130. All references in parentheses are to this edition.

8. See Andrzej Zgorzelski, "On Differentiating Fantastic Fictions: Some Supragenological Distinctions in Literature," *Poetics Today* 5. (1984): 299–307.

9. This is noted by Malcolm Bradbury in *The Modern British Novel* (Harmondsworth, U.K.: Penguin, 1994), 407–8.

Chapter 6—Brushes with History (I): *The Innocent*

1. The following reviews deal with *The Innocent:* Michael Wood, "Well Done, Ian McEwan," *London Review of Books,* 10 May 1990, 24, 26; George Stade, "Berlin Affair: A Thriller," *New York Times Book Review,* 3 June 1990, 1, 33; Julian Symons, "What to Do with the Body?" *Times Literary Supplement,* 11–17 May 1990, 497; Joan Smith, "The Body Politic," *New Statesman and Scientist,* 11 May 1990, 35–36; Anthony Burgess, "Goodbye to Berlin and Farewell to Arms," *Observer,* 6 May 1990, 61.

2. McEwan, *The Innocent* (New York: Anchor Books, 1999), 45. All references in parentheses are to this edition.

3. See, for example, Stade, "Berlin Affair," 1; and Symons, "What to Do," 497.

4. Stade, "Berlin Affair," 1, 33.

5. Wood, "Well Done," 24.

6. Smith, "The Body Politic," 36; Wood, "Well Done," 24.

Chapter 7—Brushes with History (II): *Black Dogs*

1. Billen, "A Goodbye to Gore," 28–30.

2. The following reviews deal with *Black Dogs:* Anonymous, *Observer,* 30 May 1993, 62; Graham Coster, "Evils and Novels," *London Review of Books,* 25 June 1992, 20–21; Caroline Moore, "Hounds of Hell," *Spectator,* 27 June 1992, 32; M. John Harrison, "Beating the Retreat," *Times Literary Supplement,* 19 June 1992, 20; Craig Raine, "Old Flames, New Fires," *Observer,* 29 Nov. 1992, 2; Michael Wood, "When the Balloon Goes Up," *London Review of Books,* 4 Sept. 1997, 8–9; James Saynor, "Hell in a Country Lane," *Observer,* 14 June 1992, 66; Amanda Craig, "They Rape Women," *Literary Review,* June 1992, 4.

3. McEwan, *Black Dogs* (New York: Anchor Books, 1999), xxiv. All references in parentheses are to this edition.

4. This essay has frequently been reprinted. See, for example, *Writing in a War: Stories, Poems and Essays of the Second World War,* ed. Ronald Blythe (Harmondsworth, U.K.: Penguin, 1982), 282–92.

5. Harrison notes this in his review.

6. See Joseph Conrad, *Heart of Darkness,* Part 3, in which Marlow says: "I remained to dream the nightmare out to the end, and show my loyalty to Kurtz once more."

7. Bette Pesetsky, "Irreconcilable Passions," *New York Review of Books,* 8 Nov. 1992, 7.

8. The question of fragmentariness does not arise with regard to

McEwan's first two novels, which are themselves almost the length of long short stories.

9. This concern with the past, especially with the events of the 1940s, is strongly criticized by one reviewer of *Black Dogs*. Boyd Tonkin sees it as something McEwan shares with two of his contemporaries, the novelist Martin Amis and the playwright David Hare, and as evidence of "a deep well of envy" for the "terror and glory they missed." While the concern of contemporary British novelists with the years 1939–45 is very marked, it seems rather superficial to dismiss it in this fashion. See Boyd Tonkin, "Fight Fans," *New Statesman and Society,* 19 June 1992, 26.

10. See Coster, "Evils and Novels."

11. See Saynor, "Hell in a Country Lane."

Chapter 8—Science and Fictions: *Enduring Love*

1. A number of critics have noted, some favorably, some unfavorably, the presence of scientific material in *Enduring Love*. See, for example, Merritt Moseley, "Recent British Novels," *Sewanee Review* 26. (1998): 675–82. It is worth noting that much recent British and Irish fiction does show a certain interest in science and scientific procedures.

2. De Clérambault's syndrome is authentic. Gaetan (or Gatian) G. de Clérambault (1872–1934) was a celebrated Parisian psychiatrist who described behavior that bears a close resemblance to that depicted in McEwan's novel. See Robert Jean Campbell, ed., *Psychiatric Dictionary,* 5th ed. (New York: Oxford University Press, 1981), 229–30. It is striking that McEwan depicts a homosexual and strangely unerotic case of the syndrome, (Jed seems to have no physical, sexual designs on Joe), just as he depicts a male, rather than female, victim of stalking.

3. Moseley "Recent British Novels," 679. The following reviews deal with *Enduring Love:* Anita Brookner, "Desire and Pursuit," *The Spectator,* 30 Aug. 1997, 28–29; Amanda Craig, "Out of the Balloon," *New Statesman,* 5 Sept 1997, 43; Adam Mars-Jones, "I Think I'm Right, Therefore I Am," *Observer Review,* 7 Sept 1997, 16; Jason Cowley, "Portrait: Ian McEwan," *Prospect,* Dec. 1998, 42–45; Donna Seaman, untitled, *Booklist* 94 (15 Nov. 1997): 524.

4. McEwan, *Enduring Love* (New York: Anchor Books, 1999), 108. All references in parentheses are to this edition.

5. Cowley, "Portrait: Ian McEwan," 44.

6. The novel's psychological interests are noted by several critics. See, for example, Michael Wood, "Balloon Goes Up," 8–9; and Rosemary Dinnage, "So Alert with Love," *New York Review of Books,* 9 April 1998, 32–33.

7. This is noted by Wood, "Balloon Goes Up," 8–9.

8. For some of the complexities of this and related terms one need look no further than *The New Shorter Oxford English Dictionary,* 1993 edition. See also Simon Blackburn, *Think: A Compelling Introduction to Philosophy* (Oxford: Oxford University Press, 1999), 42.

9. Oliver Reynolds, "A Master of Accidents," *Times Literary Supplement,* 12 Sept. 1997, 12.

10. This has been noticed by several critics. See, for example, Mars-Jones, "I Think I'm Right, Therefore I am."

11. See Mars-Jones, "I Think I'm Right, Therefore I am."

12. See Reynolds, "A Master of Accidents," 12.

Chapter 9—Other Works: Screenplays, the Oratorio, Children's Fiction, and *Amsterdam*

1. McEwan, *The Imitation Game: Three Plays for Television* (London: Cape, 1981), 10.

2. McEwan, *The Imitation Game,* 16.

3. Adam Mars-Jones, "Have a Heart," *Observer,* 6 Sept. 1998, 16.

4. McEwan, *The Daydreamer* (New York: Anchor Books, 2000), 9. All references in parentheses are to this edition.

5. Robert Hanks, "Flashes of Inspiration," *Independent* 12 Sept. 1998.

6. McEwan, *Amsterdam* (New York: Anchor Books, 1999), 166–68. All references in parentheses are to this edition.

7. McEwan, "The State of Fiction: A Symposium," *New Review* 5 (summer 1978): 50.

BIBLIOGRAPHY

Works by Ian McEwan

First Love, Last Rites. London: Jonathan Cape, 1975. New York: Random House, 1975.

In between the Sheets, and Other Stories. London: Jonathan Cape, 1978. New York: Simon and Schuster, 1979.

The Cement Garden. London: Jonathan Cape, 1978. New York: Simon and Schuster, 1979.

The Comfort of Strangers. London: Jonathan Cape, 1981. New York: Simon and Schuster, 1981.

The Imitation Game: Three Plays for Television. London: Jonathan Cape, 1981.

The Imitation Game and Other Plays. Boston: Houghton Mifflin, 1982.

Or Shall We Die? Words for an Oratorio Set to Music by Michael Berkeley. London: Jonathan Cape, 1983.

The Ploughman's Lunch. London: Methuen, 1985.

Rose Blanche. Pictures by Roberto Innocenti. Text by Ian McEwan, based on a story by Christophe Gallaz. London: Jonathan Cape, 1985.

The Child in Time. London: Jonathan Cape, 1987. Boston: Houghton Mifflin, 1987.

The Innocent. London: Jonathan Cape, 1990. New York: Doubleday, 1990.

Black Dogs. London: Jonathan Cape, 1992. New York: Nan A. Talese/Doubleday, 1992.

The Daydreamer. London: Jonathan Cape, 1994. New York: Harper-Collins, 1994.

Enduring Love. London: Jonathan Cape, 1997. New York: Nan A. Talese/Doubleday, 1998.

BIBLIOGRAPHY

Amsterdam. London: Jonathan Cape, 1998. New York: Nan A. Talese/Doubleday, 1998.

Critical Works about McEwan

Books

Ryan, Kiernan. *Ian McEwan*. Plymouth, U.K.: Northcote House/The British Council, 1994. Lucid chapters on McEwan's work through *Black Dogs*. Ryan is interesting on McEwan's moral vision and his relationship to feminism.

Slay, Jack, Jr. *Ian McEwan*. New York: Twayne, 1996. Clear arguments concerning McEwan's work through *Black Dogs*. Slay stresses McEwan's moral and social engagement and his focus on the importance of human relationships.

Articles and Book Sections

Annan, Gabriele. "Worriers." Review of *The Child in Time*. *New York Review*, 4 Feb. 1988, 17–19. A biting but necessary critique of McEwan's most highly regarded novel.

Bradbury, Malcolm. "Artists of the Floating World: 1979 to the Present" and "An Afterword from the 1990s (1994)." In *The Modern British Novel*, 394–462. Harmondsworth, U.K.: Penguin, 1994. A very knowledgeable summary of the main features of the fiction of McEwan and his contemporaries.

Brookner, Anita. "All Good Pals and Jolly Bad Company." Review of *Amsterdam*. *Spectator*, 12 Sept. 1998, 39. A disappointed discussion of what seems to the reviewer to be a slight text.

———. "Desire and Pursuit." Review of *Enduring Love*. *Spectator*, 30 Aug. 1997, 28–29. The distinguished author acutely analyzes Joe and praises McEwan's "clever, even brilliant novel."

BIBLIOGRAPHY

Burgess, Anthony. "Goodbye to Berlin and Farewell to Arms." Review of *The Innocent*. *Observer*, 6 May 1990, 61. An admiring and intelligent review from a major novelist.

Cowley, Jason. "Portrait: Ian McEwan." *Prospect*, Dec. 1998, 42–45. A gossipy and slightly inaccurate but interesting survey of McEwan's career. Cowley thinks the short stories are the high point.

Craig, Amanda. "They Rape Women." Review of *Black Dogs*. *Literary Review*, June 1992, 4. A negative but worthwhile review. Craig finds the novel schematic and a little ridiculous.

Dinnage, Rosemary. "So Alert with Love." Review of *Enduring Love*. *The New York Review of Books*, 9 Apr. 1998, 32–33. Very good on the love subject matter and on complexities in the narrator.

Lee, Hermione. "Shock Horror." Review of *In between the Sheets*. *New Statesman*, 20 Jan. 1978, 86–87. An important early defense of McEwan's fiction by an outstanding reviewer.

Mars-Jones, Adam. *Venus Envy*. London: Chatto and Windus, 1990. Much of this booklet is an intemperate but entertaining and telling attack on what the author sees as McEwan's hypocritical engagement with feminism.

Massie, Allan. *The Novel Today: A Critical Guide to the British Novel, 1970–1989*. London and New York: Longman/The British Council, 1990. 49–52. Clear summary of critical views on McEwan's fiction to the late 1980s from a fine novelist. Massie thinks McEwan has been overrated.

Moseley, Merritt. "Recent British Novels." *Sewanee Review* 106 (1998): 678–82. A defense of McEwan's use of scientific ideas in *Enduring Love*.

Ricks, Christopher. "Playing with Terror." Review of *The Comfort of Strangers*. *London Review of Books*, 21 Jan.–3 Feb. 1982, 13–14. A long review by a major scholar. Ricks writes about McEwan's novel in relation to a wide range of famous texts.

Spice, Nicholas. "Thatchershaft." Review of *The Child in Time*. *London Review of Books*, 1 Oct. 1987, 8–9. Good on the novel's political and social concerns.

Thwaite, Anthony. "How to Keep Mum." Review of *The Cement Garden*. *Observer*, 1 Oct. 1978, 33. An interesting article on McEwan's possible plagiarism in this novel. Praise for McEwan's technical and linguistic competence.

Wicht, Wolfgang. "Von *David Copperfield* zu Ian McEwans *The Cement Garden*: Veränderungen im Diskurs der Ich-Erzähler." *Zeitschrift für Anglistik und Amerikanistik* 36 (1988): 306–17. An interesting, if at times obscure, discussion of narration in *The Cement Garden*.

Wood, Michael. "Well Done, Ian McEwan." Review of *The Innocent*. *London Review of Books*, 10 May 1990, 24–25. A very positive and insightful review. Wood concludes that the "sheer cleverness of the book is dazzling."

———. "When the Balloon Goes Up." Review of *Enduring Love*. *London Review of Books*, 4 Sept. 1997, 8–9. A clear discussion of McEwan's philosophical concerns, both in *Enduring Love* and *Black Dogs*.

Interviews

Haffenden, John. *Novelists in Interview*, 168–90. London and New York: Methuen, 1985.

Hamilton, Ian. "Points of Departure." *New Review* 5 (autumn 1978): 9–21.

Ricks, Christopher. "Adolescence and After: An Interview with Ian McEwan." *Listener*, 12 Apr. 1979, 526–27.

INDEX